CONSOLAMINI
COMMENTARY SERIES

Commentary on Ecclesiastes and Jonah by Saint Jerome

Translated by

Robin MacGregor

Consolamini Publications

Contents

ECCLESIASTES

JONAH

Preface

This version of Jerome's Commentary on the Book of Ecclesiastes is a literal rendering of the original Latin text as set out in the Corpus Christianorum. As Jerome points out in the preface to his commentary he has tried to translate from the Hebrew and return to the original meanings, (a novel intention at the time of composition), and to compare this with the Greek versions of Symmachus, Aquila, and Theodotion. I have therefore tried to maintain the multilingual feel of the original text in preserving the original Greek words in this translation, though for the most part Jerome himself translates the meaning of these for the readers, many of whom in his day, as in ours, would not have been familiar with the specialist language..

The editorial and scriptural notes of the CCL have been preserved in this volume, as they are often very useful in enlightening Jerome's wide use of scriptural quotation and reference. As it stands the text as set out in the CCL seems to be very secure and without cause for concern. Where seemed appropriate however a different reading taken from the other available editions has been used in order to preserve what is a more suitable or likely rendition of the original meaning.

For the most part I have tried to keep to the text of the King James Version in translating Jerome's text of Ecclesiastes but where this has differed from his Vulgate edition I have always taken the latter and translated his original Latin rather than keeping to the modern text. Preference has therefore always been given to a correct rendition of the original text and commentary together.

Robin MacGregor
3rd January 2000

COMMENTARY ON ECCLESIASTES

Saint Jerome

PREFACE

I remember just five years ago when I was still at Rome[1] and studying virtuous Blesilla's book of Ecclesiastes that I taught her to think lightly of her generation and to esteem futile everything that she saw in the world. I remember too being asked by her to examine individually all the difficult passages in a short treatise so that she might be able to understand what she was reading without me always being present. Accordingly, since she was taken from us by her sudden death while I was still doing the preparation for my work, and since we, it seems, dear Paula and Eustochium, did not deserve to have such a companion in our lives, I then ceased from my work, silenced by the terrible grief of such a misfortune. Now though, situated in Bethlehem, clearly a more holy city, I can fulfil that promise to the memory of Blesilla and to you, and remind you briefly that I have used no authority in this work, but have rather translated directly from the Hebrew itself and have adapted it to the traditional language of the Septuagint in those passages which do not differ greatly from the Hebrew. Occasionally I have taken account of the Greek versions, those of Aquila, Symmachus, and Theodotion so that I do not deter the reader's enthusiasm with too much novelty. I have also not pursued those streams of conjecture, which lack a factual basis, for I do not believe this to be sensible.

1 i.e. 389 CE

1

Chapter 1

1:1 *The words of Ecclesiastes, son of David, King in Jerusalem.* The Scriptures state very clearly that Solomon was known by three names: 'Peace-making', that is 'Solomon'; 'Yedidia', that is 'beloved of Yahweh'; and the name used here 'Qoheleth', that is Ecclesiastes. He is called Ecclesiastes in Greek because he gathered together a crowd of people, *a congregation*, which we can call a demagogue because he spoke to the people and his sermon was not addressed specifically to one man but more usually to all men. Moreover he is called 'peace-making' and 'beloved of Yahweh' because there was peace during his reign and the Lord loved him. For also Psalms 44, and 71, are known by titles connected with love and peace-making. Although these psalms pertain to Christ and the Church they exhibit Solomon's joy and strength, and according to tradition were composed concerning Solomon.

He also produced an equal number of titles to the three volumes: *Proverbs*, *Ecclesiastes*, and *Song of Songs*. He teaches for children in *Proverbs* and gives instruction in the form of maxims almost with a sense of duty, and his sermons here are repeated continually to his son. In *Ecclesiastes* he teaches a man of mature age that he should not think anything in the world to be perpetual, but that all things that we perceive are in fact vain and fleeting. In *Song of Songs* he embraces an elderly man in the covenant, who has already been prepared in spurning his times. For unless we first abandon our moral failings and renounce the pomposity of our world, and prepare ourselves so we are ready for the arrival of Christ, we will not be able to say: "let him kiss me from the kiss of his mouth"[2]. Philosophers educate their followers in a manner similar to this type of instruction: first of all they teach ethics, then explain physics, and then anyone whom they see to excel in these first two they then go on to teach theology. Moreover even this should be examined more closely because Solomon is named differently in the three books. In *Proverbs* for example he is thus named: *The Proverbs of Solomon, the son of David, King of Israel.*[3] But in Ecclesiastes: *The words of Ecclesiastes, son of David, King of Jerusalem.* 'Israel' in fact is unnecessary here because it is not found in the Greek or Latin manuscripts. But in *Song of Songs* he is neither named 'son of David', not 'King of Israel' or 'King of Jerusalem', but only as *The Song of Songs of Solomon*. This is just as the Proverbs and the crude arrangement pertain to the twelve tribes and to the whole of Israel. And although the contempt of the world only comes to city-dwellers, these are the inhabitants of

2 Cant. 1,1.

3 Prov. 1,1.

2

Jerusalem, therefore Solomon intends *Song of Songs* particularly for those who desire spiritual enlightenment. To those readers just embarking on their education paternal honour and the authority of the king are claimed in their own merit, but to those who have completed their learning, and in the case where the disciple has been enlightened not by fear, but by love, his own name suffices. Then, he is equal to his teacher and he is unaware that he is a king. This is the case here. But in a more spiritual understanding Solomon was peace making and beloved of the Lord God, and Ecclesiastes can be seen as our Christ too, who destroying the inner wall and expelling evil from his flesh, makes each of them one, saying - "I give you my peace, I relinquish my peace to you"[4], about which the Lord says to his disciples "This is my chosen son whom I love: listen to him" [5], and that is he who is father of the Church. Speaking by no means to the Synagogue of the Jews but to the crowd of people the King of Jerusalem (that which was built out of the living rocks, not that about which he says "Jerusalem, Jerusalem, you that kill prophets" [6], and "Look, let your empty house be left for us" [7]), but that by which it is forbidden to swear because it is the city of a great king. This is the son of David, to whom the blind cried out in the Gospel: "pity us, son of David"; and the whole crowd sang out in unison: "Hosanna to the son of David". Then there is the fact that the word of God does not come to him as is the case with Jeremiah and the other prophets, but on account of his being rich, being a king, holding power, his wisdom and his other virtues, he speaks to the men of the church himself, and he speaks words to the apostles about which Psalm 18.5 tells us: "their sound went out to the whole world and their words went to the ends of the earth". Some scholars think wrongly, therefore, that we are tempted into desire and luxury by this book, when it teaches quite to the contrary: everything we perceive in the world is vain; nor is it fitting for us to seek those things eagerly which perish while we possess them.

1:2 ***Vanity of vanities*** said Ecclesiastes, ***Vanity of vanities, all is vanity.*** If all things that God made are truly good then how can all things be considered vanity, and not only vanity, but even vanity of vanities? Just as Song of Songs means a song that stands out from amongst all songs, so we see that in "vanity of vanities" the degree of vanity is shown. It is also written similarly in Psalm 38.6: "Nevertheless every living man is vanity." If living man is vanity

4 John 14, 27.

5 Matt. 3, 17.

6 Matth. 23, 37.

7 Matth. 23, 38

3

8 Cfr Ex. 34, 30-
35.

9 II Cor. 3, 10.

then a dead man must be vanity of vanities. We read in Exodus that Moses' face is glorified so much that the children of Israel are not able to see him[8]. Paul the apostle said that his glory was not really glory when compared to the glory of righteousness: "For even that which was made glorious had no glory in this respect, by reason of the glory that excelleth." [9] We are therefore able to say that even we in this respect, heaven, earth, the seas and all things that are contained within its compass can be said to be good in themselves, but compared to God they are nothing. And if I look at the candle in a lamp and am content with its light, then afterwards when the sun has risen I cannot discern anymore what was once bright; I will also see the light of the stars by the light of the setting sun, so in looking at the world and the multitudinous varieties of nature I am amazed at the greatness of the world, but I also remember that all things will pass away and the world will grow old, and that only God is that which has always been. On account of this realisation I am compelled to say, not once but twice: **Vanity of vanities, all is vanity.** Instead of "vanity of vanities" the Hebrew text reads 'abal abalim' which all manuscripts excepting that of the Septuagint translate similarly in Greek as *atmos atmidon* or *atmon* which we are able to translate as 'a breath' and 'a light wind which is quickly dispersed'. In this way it is shown to be vain and in no way universal by this phrase. For those things which seem to be temporal, in fact are; but those which do not are eternal. Or since that which will give rise to vanity has been exposed, he groans and is anxious and awaits the revelation of the sons of God, and "now we know in part, and we prophesy in part" [10]. All things are and will be vain, until we find that which is complete and perfect.

10 I Cor. 13, 9.

1:3 What *profit is there for a man in exchange for all his toil, which he toils under the sun?* After the general opinion that all things are vain Solomon begins to explain with regard to mankind: because men exert themselves in vain in the toil of the world, amassing wealth, teaching children, working their way towards glory, constructing buildings, and then are taken away in the midst of their work by sudden death, they hear the words: "Thou fool,

4

11 Luc. 12, 20.

this night your soul shall be required of you, then whose will be those things that you have amassed?" [11] Just as they make nothing for themselves in exchange for all this toil, so they return naked to the earth from whence they were taken.

1:4. A *generation goes, a generation comes, but the earth remains forever*. While some men die, others are born, and those you had seen, are not seen anymore, and you then see those who have not been before. What is more vain than this vanity, than that the earth remains, which was made on account of mankind? And that man himself, the master of the earth, should be suddenly returned to the dust? Another meaning of this is: the first generation of Jews dies and a generation formed from all peoples takes its place; but the earth however will remain for so long as the Synagogue's influence slips away, and the Church becomes more powerful. For when it was predicted that the Gospel would be known all around the world, then, it was said, would be the end. When the end is approaching, it is true, the sky and the earth will pass away. Solomon very precisely does not say the earth remains *through the ages*[12] but *through that age*[13]. More precisely we praise the Lord not in one age, but throughout the ages.

12 Hier.. "in saeculis"

13 Hier.. "in saeculo"

1:5. The *sun rises and the sun sets, then it rushes to its place, where it rises again*. The sun itself, which is given as light for mankind, shows the orbit of the world by its rising and it setting every day. After the sun has soaked its burning orb in the ocean, it returns by routes unknown to me to that place whence it had come; and when the period of night is over, it again bursts out quickly from its bed. In place of "rushes to its place" though, because we are following the Vulgate version, the Hebrew reads "*soeph*" which Aquila interpreted as *eispnei* in Greek, that is *pants*[14]; Symmachus and Theodotion write '*returns*' because the sun clearly turns around to its original place and it aspires to return there, from whence it had come earlier. But all of this is explained so that he can teach that with the passage of time and the rising and the setting of the stars man's age slips away and perishes, yet he does not know this for certain. Another meaning of this is: the sun of righteousness, in whose wings lies reason, rises from those who fear and sets midday in the false prophets. But when it has risen it takes us to its place. Where is that? Evidently it means to the Lord himself, for it happens that he raises us from the earth to heaven, saying, "when the son of man is lifted up, he will lift up all things to him".[15] Nor is it surprising that the son lifts up men to himself,

14 Hier.. "aspirat

15 John 12, 32.

5

when even the Lord himself lifts up to his son: "for no one", he says "comes to me except the Father, who sent me, draw him".[16] That sun therefore, which we have said sets for some and rises for other, and once set for Jacob the patriarch as he was leaving the Holy Land, rose again for him when he entered the promised land from Syria. When Lot too left Sodom and came to the city, which he was commanded to hasten to, he climbed a mountain and the sun came out above Segor[17].

1:6. It *goes to the South and rotates to the North; turning, revolving, the wind goes and returns upon its circuits.* From this we are able to believe that the sun approaches the meridian quarter in the time of winter, and in the summer is near to the Great Bear, and does not commence its movements in the equinox of autumn, but when the west wind is blowing in the time of spring, when all things give birth. But he actually says "turning, revolving, the wind goes and returns upon its circuits" as if he calls the sun itself a breath, like an animal that breathes and lives, completing its annual orbit in its course, just like the poet Vergil says: "Meanwhile the sun flies around the great year"[18] and elsewhere[19] "and the year flies through its own footsteps" or that bright sphere of the moon and Titan's star: "The breath nourishes within: and the intelligence stirs the whole mass infused through the limbs, and mingles itself with the mighty body"[20]. He is not speaking about the annual course of the sun, but its daily path. For it proceeds sidelong and towards the North, and thus turns to the East. Another meaning of this verse is: when the sun moves to the South it is closer to the Earth; when it moves to the North it is raised to higher orbits. Perhaps therefore it moves to those parts, which are compressed together by the cold of atmospheric disturbances, and of winter. Severe heat indeed blazes out from the North above the Earth, and that sun is closer to righteousness than those men who in fact live in the Northern region, and who are deprived of summer's heat. The sun then moves far away and turns by its circuits to the place whence it set out. For when it has subdued all things to it and illuminated all things with its rays, let there be the first restoration and "God may be all in all".[21] Symmachus interpreted this phrase saying, 'it goes to the meridian, and turns around to the North; turning the wind goes, and the wind returns by those routes by which it had come around'.

1:7. *All torrents flow into the sea but the sea is not filled. To the place from which the torrents come, there they return to go.* Some

16 John 6, 44

17 Cfr. Gen. 28, 11; 32, 31.

18 Aeneid 3.284

19 Vergil Georg. 2. 402.

20 Vergil Aeneid, 6. 726-7.

21 I Cor. 15, 28

6

men believe that the fresh waters that flow into the sea are either dried up by the burning sun above, or are feed for the salt-thirsty sea. Here our Ecclesiastes, the creator of the very waters, says that they return to the heads of the springs by means of hidden passages, and always boil out from their deep channels into their springs. The Hebrews believed that the rivers or sea had more significance in the metaphor of man, because they return to the earth, whence they originated. They are also called torrents not rivers because they flow that much more forcefully, yet the earth however is not filled with a great number of dead men. More precisely if we go down to the deeper parts, the turbid waters return to the sea where they used to remain. And unless I am mistaken, apart from the additions to the text, nowhere is the word 'torrent' found in a good context. For "you will drink those with the torrent of your desire" [22], although "of desire" is written in an addition. On the contrary the Saviour was taken to the brook Cedron[23], and Elisha at the time of persecution hid away in the brook of Chorat, which even dried up. But the sea is not filled up completely, in the same manner as the bloodthirsty daughters in Proverbs[24].

22 Psalms 35, 9.

23 John 18,1.

24 Prov. 30, 15.

1:8. All *things are full of toil, man cannot utter it: the eye is not satisfied with seeing, nor is the ear filled with hearing.* It is difficult to know not just about physics but also about ethics. And discourse is not able to explain the natural causes of things, nor to see those things that are hidden, (as the scope of this work demands); nor, once you have begun to learn is it possible to arrive at the greatest understanding by listening alone. For if we now look in the mirror in mystery and in part know and in part prophesy, consequently discourse will not be able to explain what it does not know; nor is the eye able to see where it is blind; nor are the ears filled by what they do not hear. At the same time this must be noted, that all words are wearying and are learnt with great difficulty, contrary to those who idly make prayers that an acquaintance with the Scriptures will come to them.

1:9. The *thing that has been, it is that which will be. And that which is done is that which shall be done. And there is no new thing under the sun.* It seems to me that he now speaks generally about those things that he enumerated above: about generation after generation, the globe of the earth, the rising and setting of the sun, the course of rivers, the vastness of the ocean and all things which we learn either through thought or through sight or hearing, because

7

25 Terence
Eunuchus, prol.
41.

26 Donatus
Comm. in
Terent. Eun

27 Origines peri
Archon III 5, 3.

there is nothing in nature that has not been before. For from the beginning of the world men have been born and have died, and the earth stood level above the waters and the sun lay in its origin. And lest I should go on to list more things, it is left to God as creator to fly with the birds, to swim with the fish, and walk with the creatures of the earth and slide with snakes. And the comic[25] said something similar to this: "Nothing has been said, which has not been said before", about which my teacher Donatus, when he was lecturing about this verse, said: "Let them die, who have said our words before us." [26] Then if is possible to say nothing new in discourse, how great the creation of the world must have been, which has been complete right from the start, that God was able to rest from his work on the seventh day! Read also in another book: "If everything that is done under the sun has already been done is past centuries, and man was already made when the sun was made: then man existed before he came under the sun."[27] But he is excluded, because by this reasoning even packhorses, gnats, and each insect and large animal is said to have been made before the sky. Unless however he should reply that talking comes from the consequences of speaking not about other animals but about the man Ecclesiastes, for he says "there is nothing new under the sun about which one can say 'look this is new!' But he does not speak of animals but of man alone, because if he means animals to be new, then he refutes his own opinion that nothing is new under the sun.

1:10. *Is there anything whereof it may be said, see this is new? It has already been for ages, which were before us.* Symmachus translated this more clearly: "Do you think there is a man who is able to say: look this is new, it has already been done before because it was before us." But he agrees with his predecessors that there is nothing new in the world, and that there is none that is able to live and say: 'look this is new', since everything that he thought he had shown to be new, already existed in former times. But we ought not to think that the signs, prodigies and the many deeds which are done for the first time by God's judgement in the world today, have already been done before in former ages, or that it was Epicurus who found this, asserting that these same things were done in innumerable periods and in these places and by these same men. Besides, both Judas betrayed *repeatedly* and Christ *often* suffered for us; and other things which have been done and will be done, are continually repeated in these times. But it could be said too, that those things, which will be done have already been done, decided out of foreknowledge and the predestination of God. For those who have been chosen in Christ before the constitution of the world existed already in previous times.

1:11. There *is no remembrance of former things; neither shall there be any remembrance of things that are to come with those that shall come after.* In the same way as the past is concealed for us in forgetfulness, thus it is with those things which are either done now, or will be done. And because of this those men who have yet to be born, will not be able to know these things, and will live life in silence, and will be obscured as if they never existed, and that verse will be fulfilled, which says, "vanity of vanities, all is vanity", for even the Seraphim, the first and last, cover up their feet on account of the appearance of God. The Septuagint is similar here: "There is no memory of former things, and even of things which are to come, there will be no memory for them with those who will come after." That is observed from the Gospel because those who were first in time are first *before all others*.[28] And because God who is benevolent and forgiving remembers all things no matter how insignificant, he will not give as much glory to those who deserve to be first on account of their faults, as he will give to those who humbly wanted to be first. And so it says consequently: "there is no memory of the wise more than of the fool for ever." [29]

28 Cfr Matth. 20, 16.

29 Eccl. 2, 16.

1:12. I, *Ecclesiastes, was King over Israel in Jerusalem.* Until now the preface has spoken only generally about all arguments; but here he returns to the subject of himself, and reveals who he was, and how he knew and experienced all things. The Hebrews say that Solomon, who was doing repentance, wrote this book, and who, having put his trust in wisdom and riches, failed God because of his wives.

30 Hier.. "in distentionem".

31 Hier.. "occupationem".

1:13. I *applied my mind to seek and probe by wisdom all that happens beneath the sky - it is a sorry task that God has given to the sons of man with which to be concerned.* Aquila, the Septuagint, and Theodotion have all translated the Hebrew word *anian* similarly as *peristasmon*, which the interpreter expressed as *occupied* in Latin[30], because the mind of man is torn asunder when occupied by several anxieties. But Symmachus uses the Greek word *ascholian*, which means business[31]. Since therefore in this book it is more often called either *occupationem*, or *distentionem*, or whatever else we have called it, they all refer to the higher senses. Ecclesiastes therefore set his mind first of all to the

9

acquisition of wisdom, and pursuing this beyond what is allowed, wanted to know the causes and reasoning why children are easily snatched by the Devil; why the righteous and the wicked are equally punished in shipwrecks; and whether these events happen as a result of fate, or by the decree of God. And if by fate, where is providence? If by decree, where is God's justice? With such desire to know these things, he said, I understand the great care and torturing anxiety experienced in many things, which was given to man by God, in order that he might desire to know that which he is not allowed to know. But the cause is inborn first, and God then gives vexation. For it is written similarly in the epistles to the Romans: "*On account of what did God give them up to the suffering of dishonour?*" [32] then again he says: "*On account of what did He give them up to uncleanness, so that they did what was not allowed*".[33] And then: "*On account of which God gave them up to desire for their uncleanness*".[34] And to the Thessalonians: "*And for this cause God will send them strong delusion.*"

[35] But the causes why they succumb were revealed earlier: either by the suffering of dishonour, or by vile affections, or by the longing in their heart, or whatever it is they do to receive strong delusion. In this way and because of their effectiveness God gave this wicked 'occupation' to man, with which to be concerned, because he did these things first voluntarily and entirely of his own will.

1:14. I *have seen all the deeds done underneath the sun, and behold all is futile and a vexation of the spirit.* We are compelled here by necessity to examine the Hebrew words more closely than we wish. It is also not possible to know the real meaning of the text, unless we learn it through studying the original Hebrew words. Aquila and Theodotion translate *routh* as the Greek *nomen*, Symmachus has *boskesin.* The Septuagint does not express the Hebrew meaning, but the Syriac, as shown in the Greek word *proairesin.* Therefore either *nome*, or *boskesis*, is the noun coming from *vexation. Proairesis* sounds more like 'will' than 'vexation'. Every single man however is said to do what he *wishes*, and what seems right to him; and men are borne with different dispositions (i.e. good and wicked) of their own free will. And all things under the sun are vain, when we displease each other by doing what is the greatest good and greatest evil. A Hebrew, who was instructing me as I read the Holy Scriptures, said to me that above the word *routh* was written "*it means rather suffering and wickedness in this place than vexation and will*", and the meaning

32 Rom. 1, 6.

33 Rom. 1, 28.

34 Rom. 1, 24.

35 II Thess. 2, 10.

10

36 Matth. 6, 34.

does not come from the evil which is contrary to good, but from that which is written in the Gospel: "*Sufficient to the day is its wickedness.*" [36] The Greeks call this more significantly *kakouchian*, so the verse essentially means: "I have considered all things, which are done in the world, and I discovered nothing except vanity and wickedness, that is distress of the soul, by which the spirit is afflicted in contrary thoughts.

1:15. A *twisted thing cannot be made straight, and what is not there cannot be numbered.* Whoever is wicked cannot be corrected, unless he was corrected beforehand. Anything that is already correct will receive embellishment; and that which is deviated will receive correction. A man is not called wrong unless he has been diverted from the correct path. This is contrary to the heretics, who entertained certain characteristics, which do not seem to be sane. And since what is missing is lacking, it cannot be numbered. Besides, only the firstborn of Israel were counted. The women, slaves, children and the people from Egypt, although of a great number, were largely overlooked, being referred to as a reduction from the army, without a number. The meaning of this can also be: such wickedness is done in the sphere of the world that the world is scarcely able to return to its completely good condition; nor is it able to regain easily its order and complete state, in which it was first created. Another meaning of this is: when all men have been restored to goodness through repentance, only the devil will remain in his wickedness. For all things which are done under the sun are done by his will and in the spirit of malevolence, while sins are piled on sins at his instigation. Then it can also mean: so great is the number of deviants and of those who have been taken away from God's flock by the devil that it is impossible to count them.

37 Cfr III Reg. 3, 5 sqq

1:16. I *said to myself: here I have acquired great wisdom, more than any of my predecessors over Jerusalem, and my mind has had much experience with wisdom and knowledge.* Solomon was not greater than Abraham and Moses, and other saints, but than those who were before him in Jerusalem. We read in the book of Kings that Solomon was very wise, and he claimed this wisdom to have been given by God before all others.[37] It was then the eye of his heart that saw great wisdom and knowledge in the world, since he does not say *I spoke much wisdom and knowledge* but *my heart saw much wisdom and knowledge.* For indeed we are not able to speak out all those things which we feel.

11

38 Horat. Epist.I, 1,41-42.

1:17. I *applied my mind to know wisdom and to know madness and folly. I perceived that this, too, is a vexation of the spirit.* Contrary abstract ideas are understood by looking at contrary facts; and " wisdom is the first to be lacking in foolishness" [38], but it is not possible to be lacking in foolishness, unless one has understood it. Many dangerous things are also created from foolishness, so that while we try to avoid them, we are actually instructed in wisdom. Solomon wanted to know wisdom and knowledge with equal enthusiasm, and equally madness and folly, so that whilst seeking some things and shunning others, his true wisdom might be proved. But in this too, as in other things, he said he found great difficulties and was not able to grasp the exact truth of matters. What I have said above about *vexation of the spirit* or *suffering of the soul*, as it is more often written in this book, should be sufficient to understand the rest of this verse.

39 Cfr Sap. 6, 7.

40 II Cor. 2, 2.

1:18. For *with much wisdom comes much grief, and he who increases knowledge increases pain.* The more a man seeks wisdom, the more he finds himself in vice and far from those virtues, which he is seeking. For those who are powerful suffer torments more gravely[39], and more is demanded of the man, to whom more is entrusted. Because of this he increases his pain who increases his knowledge, and is saddened by grief according to God, and suffers beyond his offences. The apostle said concerning this: "and who is there, who gladdens me, unless he is saddened by me?" [40] Unless perchance, and this must be understood, that a wise man would suffer so much for his wisdom, in secret and deep in his flank, nor would he show himself to prosper in intelligence, as light is to seeing; but rather through certain torments and intolerable toil, and through perpetual meditation and enthusiasm.

Chapter 2

2:1. I *said to myself: Come, I will experiment with joy and enjoy pleasure. That, too, turned out to be futile.* After I detected that pain and labour were in the essence of wisdom and the accumulation of knowledge, and nothing else except vain and endless struggle, I felt joyful that I would overflow with excess, accrue riches, amass great wealth, and take temporary pleasures before I die. But even in this I saw my vanity, for past pleasures do not help the present, and do not fill up what is empty. It is not just the pleasures of the flesh however, but also spiritual joys that are a temptation for one who possesses them. Hence I desired greatly, because I had been grabbed by this incentive and the angel of Satan too, who had knocked me down with such force that I could not recover. Solomon says about this "Don't give me riches and poverty" [1], and immediately writes underneath "lest I be full and a liar"[2], and lest I should ask, "who is looking at me?"[3], for the devil strikes down in abundance righteous men. In the apostles it is also written, "lest enraptured by his pride, he should fall into the judgement of the devil "[4], that is 'into such a judgement, as the Devil himself falls ". But having said this, spiritual joy, just as the other kinds, is claimed to be vanity, because we see it through a mirror and in mystery. But when it has been seen for what it is, then it is called vanity for no reason, but rather truth.

2:2. I *said of laughter, It is madness! And of joy, What does it accomplish?* Wherever we read *madness* the Hebrew text has *molal*, which Aquila took to be *planesin*, that is 'delusion'[5], Symmachus has *thorubon*, 'commotions'[6]. But the Septuagint and Theodotion as in many places, so too in this, also agree and translate it as *periphoran*, which we, expressing word for word, can call 'revolution'.[7] Those men therefore, who are carried around on the 'breeze' of all doctrines, are unstable and fluctuate between interpretations. Thus those who guffaw with that laugh, which the Lord says must be muted in holy weeping, are seized by the delusion of time and its whirlwind, not understanding the disaster that their sins will cause, nor bewailing their former faults, but thinking that brief joys are going to be perpetual. Then they exult in these, which are more worthy of lamentation than joy. Heretics also believe this, who agree with false doctrines and promise themselves happiness and prosperity.

1 II Cor. 12, 7

2 Prov. 30, 8.

3 Prov. 30, 9.

4 I Tim. 3, 6.

5 Hier.. "error"

6 Hier.. "tumultus".

7 Hier.. "circumlatione"

13

2:3. *I thought to stimulate my body with wine while my heart is involved with wisdom, and to grasp folly, until I can discern which is best for mankind to do under the heavens during the brief span of their lives.* I wanted to stimulate my life with enjoyment, and to lull my body, as if freed from all worries by wine, in the same way with desire; but my deep consideration and inborn reasoning, which God the creator mingled even into my sins, drew me away from the idea and led me back to seek wisdom and to spurn foolishness, so that I was able to see what was good, that men can do in the span of their lives. But he has compared desire eloquently with intoxication. Since he intoxicates and destroys the vitality of his spirit, which he was able to change into wisdom and obtains spiritual happiness, (as it is written in certain manuscripts), he is able to discern which things ought to be sought out in this life, and which avoided.

2:4. *I acted in grand style: I built myself houses, I planted vineyards;* and others such until the point where he says: *The wise man has his eyes in his head, whereas the fool walks in darkness.* Before I discuss each of these in turn it seems useful to me to encompass all of them in a short paragraph, and to reduce their meanings to just one explanation, so that it is easier to understand what is being said. I had all things that have been considered good through the ages. I built myself a palace on high, and covered the hills and mountains with vines. And lest anything be lacking from my excess I planted gardens and orchards of different kinds of trees, which were watered from above by water stored in pools, so that the growth was fed for longer periods with continual moisture. I also had an uncountable number of slaves, buyers and natives, and many flocks of animals, cows of course, and sheep- no king before me in Jerusalem had such a number. I also amassed a huge number of treasure houses of gold and of silver, which I obtained as gifts from various kings and as tributes from conquered races. And because of this it happened that I was prompted by having too much wealth to even more pleasures, and they called to me in choirs of music, flutes, lyres and in songs, and each sex served in entertainment. Those temptations grew in such quantity as I was lacking in wisdom. For desire had dragged me to each and every pleasure and I was being carried along unbridled and headlong, and I thought that that was the fruit of my labours, if I myself was consumed with lust and luxury. Having then at last returned to my senses, and as if waking from a deep sleep, I looked at my hands and saw that my work was full of vanity, full of squalor, and full of the character of my folly. For I found nothing to be good that was considered good in

14

the world. Considering therefore those things which were good for wisdom and which were bad for foolishness I rushed to praise any man, who then refrained from his sins and was able to pursue true virtues. Certainly there is a great diversity between wisdom and foolishness, and virtues are as much separated from vices as day differs from night. It seems to me then that he that follows that path of wisdom always lifts his eyes to heaven and raises his face aloft, and considers those things which are above his head; but he that gives in to foolishness and vices fumbles in the darkness and flounders in his ignorance of the world. *I acted in grand style: I built houses for myself, I planted vineyards.* He, who is raised up equal to the face of God in the heavens, makes his work great; and he builds houses so that the Father and the Son will come, and will live in them. And he plants vineyards to which Jesus will tie up his ass.

2:5. *I made for myself gardens and orchards and planted in them every kind of fruit tree.* In my treasure house are not only gold and silver dishes but even some that are made from wood and pottery. And even the gardens therefore are made on account of certain weaker and sick men, for anyone who is sick will eat vegetables. Trees are planted, not all of them fruit-bearing as we have in the Latin manuscripts, but of all fruits, that is of varied fruits and fruit-trees, because the grace of the Church is also varied. Thus one type of tree is the eye, one the hand and another the foot, and on those things which are most prized we bestow our greatest glory. And amongst those fruit-trees I esteem the wood itself to be primal in life because it is wisdom, for unless that is planted in their midst the other trees will dry up.

2:6. *I constructed pools from which to irrigate a grove of young trees.* The wood in glades and in forests, which is not fruit-bearing, are not nourished by rain from the sky, not by such rain waters but by water which is collected in pools from rivers. Even low-lying Egypt is situated low in the land like a vegetable patch, and is irrigated by waters, which come from Ethiopia. But the Promised Land which is mountainous and raised up waits for timely or late-coming rain from the sky.

2:7. *I bought slaves, male and female, and natives too; I also owned more possessions, both cattle and sheep, than all of my predecessors in Jerusalem.* If we want Ecclesiastes, as we have

8 Hier..
"animas"

said before, to refer to the person of Christ here too, then we are able to say *his slaves* who have the spirit of fear in servitude and desire more spiritual things in life than they already have. But we can also call the slave-girls *hearts*[8] that till now have been bestowed upon the body and upon the earth. They surpass also those natives, who are certain of the Church, both slaves and slave-girls, about whom I have spoken. And the Lord has not yet bestowed upon them freedom or noble-birth. But there are others in the estate of Ecclesiastes like oxen and sheep, who are kept on account of work and their innocence, and who work even in the church without reason and knowledge of the Scriptures. But they have not yet attained such an understanding, that they deserve to be men and return to the appearance of their creator. If you look more diligently too, you will notice that the number is not added in the case of slaves, slave-girls and natives, but in the case of cows and sheep it is said: "I owned more possessions of cattle and sheep". There is more silver in fact in the Church than men: more sheep than slaves, slave-girls and natives. But that which is said at the end- "more than all those who were before me in Jerusalem" does not pertain to the glory of Solomon, or that he was richer than his father the King, since Saul did not rule in Jerusalem, and the city was held by the Jebusites who had themselves occupied the city at that time. Ecclesiastes however was richer at a younger age than were all men, who had preceded him as kings in Jerusalem.

2:8. I *amassed even silver and gold for myself, and the treasure of kings and the provinces; I provided myself with various singers and musical instruments, and with every human luxury- chests and chests of them.* Divine scripture always places silver and gold above speech and meaning. The dove in the sixty-seventh Psalm represents this too, which is interpreted as a spirit, and is more noticeable because of its silver wings, so that it hides the underlying significance of the pallor of gold. But he gathers the treasures of kings and of the provinces or kingdoms into the Church of believers. He refers to those kings about whom the psalmist writes "the kings of the earth were there and the chiefs gathered together"[9]. And he refers to those kingdoms to which the Saviour orders us to raise our eyes[10], since now they burn with fear. The treasures of kings can be called both the doctrines of philosophers and also secular knowledge[11], which Ecclesiastes understands

9 Ps. 2, 2.

10 Cfr John 4.

11 Cfr I Cor. 1.

16

well: he takes hold of the wise men in their wisdom, and squanders the wisdom of the wise, and reproves the discretion of the prudent. The choirboys and girls are those who sing with vitality and with intelligence. A male singer sings like a man who is both strong and spiritual about heavenly matters. But a girl flits about the matter, which the Greeks call *hulen*. Nor is she able to raise her voice loudly into the air. Therefore wherever a woman is mentioned in the Scriptures and the weaker sex, we are to translate it according to an understanding of the context. Pharaoh does not want the male children to be allowed to live for example, but only the females in this matter.[12] And another point is that none of the saints is said to have had a daughter[13], and it is only Salphaat, who died for his sins, that had all girls. Jacob is the father of one daughter amongst the twelve patriarchs, but is endangered by her.[14] The pleasures also of mankind over wisdom must be understood, which have many fruits and desires like paradise. We are admonished against them, saying, "take delight in the Lord and he will give you the request of your heart"[15], and in another place, "you will drink them as the torrent of your desire".[16] (I had wanted to shun reference to the female sex, and even now use the distinction of the male, because the Latin language does not take readily to this.) Aquila explains about the wine-pourers, male and female, in a manner very different to the fashion written here. For Solomon is not naming the sexes of man, clearly either male or female, but types of dish, and he calls them *kulikion* and *kulikia*, which is written in Hebrew as *sadda* and *saddoth*. Then Symmachus, who was not able to express the idea word for word, translates this in a similar way: *types of table and equipment*. Therefore Solomon is believed to have had either pitchers, wine goblets, or bowls arranged in chests, and which were ornate with gold and with jewels. And he drank from a *kulikio* in one, (that is, a bowl) and from *kilikiois* in other places, which are clearly smaller dishes; and the crowd of drinkers received wine at the hands of his servants. Because we explain Ecclesiastes as being Christ, therefore wisdom, having mingled her wine (as it says in Proverbs) calls out to those who wander to come to her. [17] Now we must see the body of the Lord as a very great bowl, in which is

12 Cfr Ex. 1, 16.

13 Cfr Num. 26,32 ; 27, 3.

14 Cfr Gen. 30, 21 ; 34.

15 Ps. 36, 4.

16 Ps. 35, 9.

17 Cfr Prov. 9, 2.3.

17

not pure divinity as there is in heaven, but there God is blended with humanity on account of us, and wisdom is then poured out by the apostles to smaller *kulikia*, small goblets and bowls held by believers throughout the world.

2:9. Thus *I grew and surpassed any of my predecessors in Jerusalem; still, my wisdom stayed with me.* It seems to me that Ecclesiastes, acting grandly, agrees less with the Lord, unless by chance we adapt this to him: "He [Jesus] increased in wisdom and age and grace"[18]. And, "on account of which God took him on high[19]". He also says "those who were before me in Jerusalem" and is referring to those who, before he arrived, steered the congregation of holy men and the Church. If we explain the text in a spiritual way then Christ is richer than all men; and he only perceives the Synagogue better in bodily form than the Church. Therefore he wears a veil, because it was placed over the face of Moses and he let us see his face in daylight.[20] More precisely "wisdom has stayed with me", means even in respect to the temptations of the body wisdom stayed with him. For he who receives a profit from his wisdom will not keep wisdom long, but he who does not receive a gain, nor grows through change, but always has plenty- he is able to say, "and wisdom has stayed with me".

2:10. Whatever *my eyes desired I did not deny them; I did not deprive myself of any joy. Indeed my heart drew joy from all my activities, and this was my reward for all my endeavours.* The eyes of the heart and the sight of the mind desire to gaze on spiritual matters, which the sinner does not see, so forbids his heart from true happiness. Therefore Ecclesiastes gave himself completely over to this cause and balanced eternal glory lightly in an world of discord. This is our lot, and our continual reward if we work for our virtues.

2:11. Then *I looked at all things that I had done and the energy I had expended in doing them.* He who does all things with diligence and wariness is able to say this. *It was clear that it was all futile and a vexation of the spirit, [and there is no profit under the sun.]* As if he considers that in comparison with other things, all things are cheap which are under the sun, and are different according to the variety of desires. *And there is no profit under the*

18 Luc. 2, 52.

19 Phil. 2, 9.

20 Cfr Ex. 34,33. ; II Cor. 3, 13.

18

sun. Christ placed his tabernacle in the sun. So Christ will not be able to live, nor be plentiful in whoever has not yet obtained the lucidity of the sun, its regularity and constancy.

2:12. *Then I turned my attention to appraising wisdom with madness and folly - for what can man who comes after the king do?* This seems to discuss heavenly matters until the place where he says, "the eyes of a wise man are in his head". I had summed up all things in one explanation, intending to show the meaning briefly, and because of that, again according to *anagoge*[21], I had only touched lightly on some things, but now I ought to explain in a manner similar to that in which I began. For the meaning is quite different here from the interpretation found in the Septuagint. But he says he had returned to seeking wisdom after pleasures and those desires he had condemned, in which he found more foolishness and stupidity than true and recognised knowledge. For man, he said, is not able to know so clearly and truly the wisdom of his creator and of his king, as his creator knows it himself. And so he says that those things that we know, we only think we have grasped and value more than know what is true.

2:13. And *I perceived that wisdom excels folly as light excels darkness.* I am allowed, he says, to see through that very wisdom of mankind, which is mixed with uncertainty. Nor is it possible, he adds, for it to flow into our minds so clearly as it does into the king and our creator. I know however that the difference between wisdom and folly is great even as much as one can differentiate between day and night, between light and dark.

2:14. The *wise man has his eyes in his head, whereas a fool walks in darkness. But I also realised that the same fate awaits them all.* Whoever attains complete wisdom and has deserved Christ to be his aim always raises his eyes to the heavens and will therefore never think about terrestrial matters. When these things are considered in this way and there is such a distinction between a wise man and a fool, one being compared with day and the other with darkness, the former raises his eyes to heaven, the latter looks on the ground. Suddenly this thought occurred to me, why both the wise man and the fool are constrained by a common mortality - why the same wounds, the same fate, the same death and equal troubles confine each one.

21 Allegorical interpretation bearing out a deeper sense of the Scriptures.

19

2:15/16. *So I said to myself: the fate of the fool will befall me also; to what advantage then have I become wise? But I concluded that this, too, was vanity. For there is no comparison between the remembrance of the wise and of the fool at all, for as the succeeding days roll by, is all forgotten? How can the wise man's death be like the fool's?* I have stated that the wise man and the fool, the righteous and wicked are destined to die by the same fate and all wicked things in this world will suffer a similar fate; what profit is there for me then, that I have sought wisdom and worked more than others? On reconsidering the matter and applying myself to it diligently I saw that my opinion was unfounded. For the wise and foolish will not have similar remembrance in the future when the end of the world comes; and they will be confined for no reason by equal death because the wise man will continue to the joys of heaven and the fool to his punishment. The Septuagint translates the meaning of the Hebrew here more clearly, for it doesn't necessarily follow the Hebrew word order: "and to what purpose have I become wise?" Then I said to myself copiously, (for the fool is he, who speaks too much), 'for this is also vanity, because there is no remembrance of the wise with the fool for ever, and so on.' Since he tried to convince us that his prior thoughts were foolish, he bore witness that he had spoken foolishly, and that he had erred, and it was by doing this that he realised his folly.

2:17. So *I hated life, for I was depressed by all that goes on under the sun, because everything is vain and a vexation of the spirit.* The world has been given over to unkindness[22] and the apostle moans about the tabernacle saying "I am a wretched man, who will free me from the body of this death?"[23], and he hates quite rightly everything that is done under the sun. That is however only in comparison with paradise and the beatitude of that life, in which we would enjoy the fruits of wisdom and the pleasures of virtues. But now as if we are in a prison camp or cell, and with a wall of tears, we eat our bread in the sweat of our brow.

2:18/19. *Thus I hated all my achievements labouring under the sun, for I must leave it to the man who succeeds me. And who knows whether he will be wise or foolish? - And he will control all my possessions which I toiled and have shown myself wise under the sun. This, too, is vanity.* He seems to be reconsidering wealth and riches, because according to the Gospel, being snatched by sudden death, we do not know with which kind of heir we die -

22 Cfr I John. 5, 19.

23 Rom. 7, 24.

20

whether he will be a fool or wise who will enjoy the fruits of our toil. This was also the case with Solomon: for he did not regard his son Roboam as similar to himself. We learn from this that a son is not worthy of his father's heredity if he is foolish. But to me studying the work it seems that he is speaking more about spiritual labour, because a wise man will work on the Scriptures for days and nights, and will compose books and will hand down his memory to his descendants, and nonetheless all this will come into the hands of fools, who repeatedly find in them the seeds of heresy, according to the perversity of their own mind, and waste other men's efforts. For if the text now refers to Ecclesiastes' personal wealth, it was necessary to say about toil and wealth: "and he will control all my possessions which I toiled and have shown myself wise under the sun." For what is wise in the pursuit of earthly riches?

2:20/23. *So I turned my heart to despair of all that I had achieved by toiling under the sun. For there is a man who laboured with wisdom, knowledge and skill, yet he must hand on his portion to one who has not toiled for it. This too is vanity and a great evil. For what has a man in return for all his toil and his stress, which he toils beneath the sun? For all his days are painful, and his business is a vexation; even at night his mind has no rest. This, too, is vanity!* Previously he has spoken about the uncertainty of an heir and not knowing whether he will be foolish or wise, the master of the works of another. But even now he seeks the same things but this time the meaning is different, because he might leave his wealth and labours perhaps to his son, to a neighbour, or someone he knows. Nevertheless it happens time and time again that one man enjoys in the work of another, and *sweet toil is to the dead while pleasures are for the living.* He thinks of himself as every single one and he will see with how much toil he composes his books, how "often he turns his pen, again he will write those things which are worthy of law"[24], and for the man who does not work he will give him his own share. For what good to the wealth of the earth, as I have said clearly, are wisdom, knowledge and virtue, in which he said he had laboured? For although he may be virtuous, wise and knowledgeable he spurns worldly things.

2:24/26. *Is it not good for man that he eats and drinks and shows his soul satisfaction in his labour? And even that, I perceived, is from the hand of God. For who should eat and who should make haste except me? To the man who pleases Him He has given wisdom, knowledge and joy; but to the sinner He has given the*

24 Horat. Sat. I. 10, 72/73.

21

urge to gather and amass - that he may hand it on to one who is pleasing to God. That, too, is vanity and a vexation of the spirit. After I examined all things and saw that nothing was more unjust than one man enjoying the work of another, then this work seemed to me to be the most righteous, and like a gift of God, seeing that a man may enjoy his own labour, drinking and eating, and for a time refraining from amassed wealth. And sometimes it is a gift of God, that such a mind as is bestowed upon righteous men, that they squander those things, which they have sought with great attention and vigilance. In fact on the other hand, it is the character of the anger of God, which is set against the sinner, so he amasses wealth day and night and uses if for no purpose, then he bequeaths it to those men who are righteous in the sight of God. But, he says, looking at this more closely and noticing that all things come to a common end with death, I have judged it to be the most vain of all. These readings are very close to the text though, so that I do not seem to completely miss the plain meaning of the words, and while I follow spiritual riches, disdain the poverty of history. For what is good then, or what kind of gift of God is it, either to covet his wealth and like a man in flight gather desire prematurely, or to turn someone else's work to ones own pleasures, and then to think that this is a gift of God, if we take pleasure in others' discomfort and toil? It is good though, to take our own food and drink, which we have found by divine will, from the flesh and blood of a Lamb. For who is either able to eat or when there is need to spare in the absence of God? He warned that sacred food must not be given to the dogs[25], and he teaches how rations ought on occasion to be given to slaves[26], and similar to another meaning, that is we ought to eat only honey that has been found, and only as much as is needed. But God gives wisdom and knowledge and happiness to the man who is good.[27] For unless he was good and corrected his ways beforehand by his own judgement, he will not be worthy of that wisdom, knowledge and happiness, according to that which is said in another place: "Plant for yourselves in justice, make a vintage of the fruit of life, enlighten for yourselves the light of knowledge."[28] In fact, righteousness ought to be planted first, and the fruit of life must be reaped, only then, afterwards the light of knowledge will be able to appear. Therefore just as God gave the good man wisdom and other gifts, in the same way he has forsaken the sinner according to his own judgement, and made him amass riches and contrive false doctrines therefrom. When a saintly man who is pleasing to God sees these things, he understands them, since they are vain and composed of the conceit of the spirit. Nor should we admire what he

25 Cfr Matth. 7, 6.

26 Cfr Matth. 24, 45.

27 Cfr Prov. 25, 16.

28 Os. 10, 12. (as in LXX)

22

has said: "he gave vexation to the sinner" and so on. For this must be seen in concordance with that meaning which I have often explained: that for this reason anxiety or vexation has been given to him, since he was a sinner, and the cause of vexation was not in God, but in himself, who had sinned previously by his own volition.

Chapter 3

3:1. Everything *has its season, and there is a time for everything under the heavens.* He has taught in the previous verses the doubtful and changeable state of humanity; now he wants to show that all things are opposed to each other in the world, and that nothing remains forever of those things, which are under the heavens and beyond time, since the other spiritual substances are contained neither in the heavens nor in time.

3:2. A *time to be born and a time to die. A time to plant and a time to uproot that which has been planted.* No one doubts that men are born and die, and God knows that what he has planted will grow full and well; for to pull out what has been planted is to die. But since we read in Isaiah[1] "we have conceived, laboured with and given birth out of a fear for You", this must be said, because when a man is ready, that man in particular, who was born from fear, will die as soon as he has begun to love God. Since indeed "perfect love sends fear outside"[2]. The Hebrews understand all that he has written about the contradiction of times, (until it says " a time for war and a time for peace") as concerning Israel. Because it is not necessary to go through each verse in turn here, commenting on how they are to be interpreted and what they mean, I will list them briefly, leaving a more detailed study to the reader's discretion. There was a time for growing and planting in Israel, a time for dying and leading it into bondage. A time for killing them in Egypt, and a time for freeing them from Egypt. A time for destroying the Temple under Nebuchadnezer, and a time for rebuilding under Darius. A time for bewailing the plundering of the city and a time for laughing and dancing under Zorobabel, Esdra, and Nehemiah. A time for dissemination from Israel and a time for gathering them together again. A time like a belt or harness put around the Jews by God, and a time for leading them into bondage in Babylon and there for them to rot across the Euphrates. Read *perizoma* of Jeremiah[3]. A time for seeking them out and rescuing, a time for losing and a time for forsaking. A time for schism in Israel and a time for reunification. A time for hushing the prophets, now when in Roman bondage and a time for proclaiming them aloud, when even in enemy lands they weren't lacking in God's presence or comfort. A time for loving, in which He loved those men before our fathers, a time for hating, since they threw their hands up against Christ. A time for war, only not for those who are doing repentance for

1 Is. 26, 18.

2 I. John. 4, 18.

3 Cfr Ier.. 13, I-II.

24

themselves and a time for peace in the future, when all the tribes return, and all Israel will be safe.

3:3. A *time for killing and a time for healing.* It is both the time for killing and the time for healing, he says: "I will kill, and I will revive"[4]. He cures, provoking one to repentance. 'I killed' has the same meaning as "in the morning I murdered all the sinners of the Earth."[5] *A time for destroying and a time for building.* We are not able to build anything good unless we have first destroyed what is bad. Just as the word of Jeremiah came from God so that he first rooted out, undermined and killed; then he built and planted.[6]

3:4. A *time for weeping and a time for laughter.* Now is the time for weeping and in the future it will be the time for laughter: for "the blessed weep, since they themselves will laugh."[7] *A time for bewailing and a time for dancing.* For this reason they are seized in the Gospel, those to whom God says " I have lamented for you and you have not moaned; I sang and you did not dance."[8] We must moan at present so that afterwards we can dance that dance, which David danced before the arc of the covenant[9], and displeasing to the daughter of Saul he was more pleasing to God.

3:5. A *time for dispersing stones and a time for collecting stones.* I marvel how an learned man could have said this ridiculous note about this passage: "this passage speaks about the destruction and killing of Solomon's houses, because men first destroy, then build". Some amass stones to construct buildings, others destroy those buildings which have been erected, according to Horace's lines "he demolished, he builds, exchanges squares with wheels, he fluctuates and disagrees with the whole order of life itself." [10] Whether he is correct in saying this or not I leave up to the reader to decide. Nonetheless we should follow the sequence of the prior explanation-they say it is a time for scattering and collecting stones, similar to what is written in the Gospel: "God is powerful enough to raise up the sons of Abraham from these stones".[11] For there was a time for dispersing the nation and a time for gathering them again into the Church. I have read in a certain book, (like the Septuagint however, which says "there was a time for throwing stones and a time for collecting them") that the harshness of the ancient law of the Gospel was tempered by grace. In fact the stern law, unkind and unforgiving, murders the sinner, he pities with the

4 Deut. 32, 39.

5 Ps. 100.8.

6 Ier.. I, 10.

7 Luc. 6, 21.

8 Luc. 7, 32.

9 Cfr II Reg. 6, 14.

10 Horat. Epist. I. I. 100, 99.

11 Matth. 3, 9.

25

grace of the Gospel and provokes men to repentance. And there is a time for throwing stones, or collecting them, because stones are thrown in law and are collected in the Gospel. Whether this is true fact or not is credited to the author.

A time for embracing and a time for being far from embrace. The meaning of this is seemingly the simplest understanding- the apostle agrees with the same words: "do not cheat each other, unless by chance it is agreed for a time that you give yourselves to fasting and to prayer."[12] Attention must be given to children, and again to self-control. Or perhaps it was the time for embrace when the opinion was flourishing that we ought to "grow and multiply, and fill up the Earth"[13]. And the time became far from one of embracing when it passed away: "the times are hard; it remains that both they that have wives be as though they had none".[14] But if we wanted to climb to the higher parts, we would see wisdom embracing its lovers: for he says "honour it and it will embrace you"[15], and hold them in its arms and lap in a tighter embrace. More precisely, it is not always possible to stretch the human mind to heaven and think about the divine and higher things, or continually consider celestial matters, but meanwhile to indulge in the necessities of the flesh. On account of this there is a time for embracing wisdom, and holding it more tightly, and a time for relaxing the mind from the study and embrace of wisdom, just as of the care of the body, and we have those things that our life needs in the absence of sin.

3:6/7. *A time to acquire and a time to lose. A time to keep and a time to throw away.* As is in many verses before the meaning is the same here too, which is apparent before and following this verse, in that he says: *A time to destroy and a time to build.* And then *A time to rend and a time to mend.* Just as the Synagogue is destroyed so that the Church can be built and schism is only brought about by the law so that the Gospels are unified, because each preacher has carried it out one by one, unifying from the law and the prophets the testimonies of the arrival of the Lord. And thus there was a time for seeking and guarding Israel, a time for losing and discarding it. Or perhaps in fact a time for seeking a nation in the tribes and a time for losing the people of the Jews. A time for guarding the believers of the nations and a time for dismissing the faithless from Israel. *A time for silence and a time for speaking.* I think that the Pythagoreans, whose discipline is to remain silent for five years and afterwards to speak to learned men, took the origin of

12 I Cor. 7, 5.

13 Gen. 1, 28.

14 I Cor. 7, 29.

15 Prov. 4, 8

26

their decree from this. Let us learn therefore and so remain silent first, so that afterwards we open our mouths only to speak. Let us be silent for a set period and depend on the utterances of our teacher. Nothing seems right to us unless we learn that after much silence we are made into teachers by our pupils. Now though instead of the world slipping day by day into a far worse situation, we teach in churches what we do not know. And if by composing words or at the bidding of the devil, who is the patron of madness, we have aroused the applause of the common people, then we think we understand, (contrary to our conscience), what it is we were able to dissuade others from. We do not learn all the arts without a teacher, only those which are so common and easy that they don't require a tutor.

3:8. A *time for loving and a time for hating.* The time for loving God, children, wife, and relatives is afterwards, and the time for hating those in martyrdom since hostile piety attacks those steadfast men for the sake of the confession of Christ. Or maybe there is a time for loving the law, and those things that the law decrees- that is circumcision, sacrifices, the Sabbath, Neumania[16], and a time for hating them when the grace of the Gospel has been lost. But we cannot say this, since now we look through the mirror in mystery, the time for loving is the present, and in the future there will come a time when we will see face to face and then, more accomplished, we will begin to hate and despise what we love.[17] *A time for war and a time for peace.* Although we are in the present world, it is the time for war: when we have left this world the time for peace will come. For the place of God is in peace and so too is our city of Jerusalem, for it is called 'chosen in peace'. Therefore no one now thinks he is safe: you must prepare yourselves in the time of war and put on the apostles arms, so that we may rest in peace at last victorious.

3:9/11. *What gain, then, has the worker in exchange for all his toil? I have observed the task which God has given the sons of man to be concerned with: He made everything beautiful in its time; He has also put an enigma into their minds so that man cannot comprehend what God has done from the beginning to end.* The opinion of many other scholars on this passage does not escape me, because in this world God conceded to the teachers of perverse doctrines their true occupation, lest man's idle mind should become slow and while thinking that God's creations are good, yet nonetheless not be able to see them as the natural knowledge of the

16 The Jewish feast of the New Moon.

17 Cfr I Cor. 13, 12.

world. But the Hebrew who taught me the Scriptures explained it in this way: when all things are placed in their own time and there is a time for destroying or building, weeping and laughing, silence and speaking, and others things which are said about time, why do we try to survive in vain and believe the labours of this short life to be perpetual? And according to the Gospel we are not even happy, and it is called wickedness since we think nothing of tomorrow.[18] For what more are we able to have inthis world than continual striving in that toil, which God has given to man, so that one man may gain more by following others, in a situation where he is able to learn and exercise himself? For all that God does is good, but good in his world. It is good to wake and to sleep, but it is not good to be always awake or asleep, since in turn each and every thing can be considered good, when there is need, according to God's plan. Moreover God also created the world to be inhabited by men, so that they should enjoy the variation of time, and not seek the causes of nature, how all things are made, why He made this or that grow or change from the beginning of the world until now.

3:12/13. *Thus I perceived that there is nothing good for each of them than to rejoice and do what is good in his life. Indeed every man who eats and drinks and finds satisfaction in all his labour- it is a gift from God.* Therefore the settler and the foreigner of the world has been charged that he should enjoy the time of his short life, and when the hope of a longer life has been removed, he sees everything that he has as if he is about leave this life, and he sees also what he can do well in his life. And his thoughts are not in vain thus twisted, on account of his amassed wealth. And he doesn't think that he is able to acquire more from his toil than his food and drink and if he expends anything from his wealth into good work, then only this is a gift of God. We are not provoked, as some scholars think, by such words into luxury, pleasures, and desperation as are animals, according to that phrase of Isaiah: "let us gorge ourselves and drink, for tomorrow we will die."[19] But according to the apostle: "having sustenance and clothing, we are content with these."[20] And whatever we have that is more than this, we use in feeding the poor and our need for charity. More to the point, since the true food is the flesh of the Lord, and his blood is the true drink, according to *anagoge*[21], we only regard this as good in the present world, if we actually do feed from his flesh and drink from his blood, not only in secret but even in reading the Scriptures. For true food and drink, which is taken from the word of God, is knowledge of the Scriptures. But no one believes the word of Balaam of the

18 Cfr Matth. 6, 34.

19 Is. 22, 31.

20 I Tim. 6, 8.

21 See footnote 60.

22 Num. 23, 23.

23 Cfr Eccl. 3, 13.

24 Luc. 6, 21.

25 Cfr Iob. 8, 21.

prophets, who says "there will be no toil against Jacob, no suffering in Israel"[22]. It is in fact contrary to this, because it is said to be a gift of God: "If anyone eats and drinks and shows he is good in all of his work"[23]. In fact these are the many troubles of the righteous. And the apostle complains about these, saying he has sweated in toil and suffering. But the Lord freed us for our future in toil and suffering also: "there will be no toil against Jacob, no suffering in Israel". And we read how " the blessed weep, since they will laugh"[24], and our laughter follows the words of Job the prophet: for the "mouth will be filled with the joy of truths"[25]. Thus now we enjoy our toil in good work, by which we restrict and restrain ourselves so that afterwards we may cease from working.

3:14. I *realised that whatever God does will endure forever: nothing can be added to it and nothing taken away, and God has acted so that man should fear Him.* There is nothing in the world that is new. The course of the sun and moon in turn and the dryness and verdure of the earth and trees are born and take shape with the world itself. And therefore God governed all things by a defined plan and commanded the elements to be at the disposal of man, for his use, so that when men see these things they know that there is providence and fear the appearance of God; while from the equality of the world, the natural season, order, and constancy they understand their creator. "For his invisible work in the creation of the world are clearly seen, being understood by the things which are made, even his eternal virtue and power"[26]. If we want we can

26 Rom. 1, 20.

read this as if from the beginning, with the meaning of the first part already understood: "and God has acted so that man should fear Him" then this is the meaning: God made all these things, so that men fear him, and reject for another what God once created for

27 Ps. 33, 17.

man. But he governed perfectly, saying: "so that they should fear his appearance".[27] The image of the Lord, indeed, is powerful over those who are wicked.

3:15. What *has been, already exists, and what is still to be, has already been, and God seeks him that suffers persecution.* All things we perceive in the past, present or future, they themselves have been, are, and will be. That same sun which now rises, existed before we were in this world, and after we die, it will rise again. But we have mentioned the sun, so that we understand other things to be the same as they have been before. Because if they are seen to die by what we call death, they do not really die, but grow again given a

29

second life, and nothing dies forever but is reborn and relives as if with a certain new seed. For this is what he says: "and God seeks him that suffers persecution", which is said better in Greek *kai ho theos zetesei to diokomenon* that is what dies, what has perished, and has ceased to be. But if that speaks about all that are in the world there is no doubt about man, that having died he will be reborn. But if anyone likes to choose a beginning as if his own, "and God seeks him that suffers persecution", he uses this evidence in the persecution of certain people: to comfort him, who had persevered in martyrdom. And since all in this world, who want to live religiously, follow the apostle, they suffer persecution and take consolation in the fact that God seeks him that suffers persecution, just as he seeks out the blood of a man who has been murdered, and comes to seek what has perished, and carry the wandering sheep back to the flock on his shoulders.[28]

28 Cfr Luc. 19, 10 ; 15, 4-7.

3:16/17. *Furthermore, I have observed beneath the sun: in the place of justice there is wickedness, and in the place of righteousness there is wickedness. I mused: God will judge the righteous and the wicked, for there is a time for everything and for every deed, there.* The meaning of this is clear but is cloaked by the cloud of interpretation. He says: I sought truth and righteousness under the sun and I saw that even among the benches of judges truth is not valued, but gifts. Or differently: I thought some kind of justice present in this world and either took the pious man on his own merit, or punished the impious for his crimes; and I found the opposite to that which I had been thinking. For I saw a righteous man here suffer much injustice and an impious man made to rule instead of being punished for his crime. But thinking to myself afterwards and considering it carefully I understood that they judge not in respect of God and treating each case one by one, but rather reserve judgement for the future, so that all are judged equally and receive there according to their will and effort. For this is what he says: "and there is a time for everything and for every deed, there", that is, in judgement when God will have begun to judge, then there will be truth, now injustice prevails in the world. Such as when we read in Wisdom, Sirach wrote: "lest you say, what is this or what is that? For all things are sought in their own time"[29].

29 Eccli. ?

3:18/21. *Then I said to myself concerning men: God has chosen them out, but only to see that they themselves are as beasts. For the fate of men and the fate of beast - they have one and the same fate: as one dies so the other dies, and they all have the same*

30 cfr Gen. 37, 35 ; 42, 38 ; 44, 31.

31 cfr Iob. 7, 9 ; 17, 13.16.

32 cfr Luc. 16, 26.

33 A long missile weapon of barbarian nations.

34 Gen. 3.19.

spirit. Man has no superiority over beast, for all is futile. All go to the same place; all originate from dust and return to dust. Who perceives that the spirit of man is the one that ascends on high while the spirit of the beast is the one that descends down into the earth? It is not surprising that there is no distinction in this life between righteous and wicked, nor that none values virtues, but all things occur with uncertain outcome, where nothing seems to differ according to the worthlessness of the body between sheep and men: there is the same birth, common end in death; we proceed similarly towards the light and are equally dissolved into the dust. But there seems to be this difference, that the spirit of man ascends to the heavens, and the spirit of animals goes down into the earth, but from where do we know this for certain? Who can know whether what is hoped is true or false? But he says this, not because he thinks the spirit dies with the body, or that there's one place set aside for beasts and for man, but because before the arrival of Christ all were led equally to the nether regions. Jacob said that he was about to go down to those regions.[30] And Job complains that the pious and impious are held back in the lower world.[31] And the Gospel says that with an abyss blocking the way even Abraham and Lazarus were rich in prayers in the underworld.[32] And in fact before Christ accompanied by a robber opened the wheel of flames, and the fiery rumpias[33] and the gates of paradise, the heavens were closed and the equal unworthiness of the spirits of sheep and of men was abridged. One also seems to be dispersed and the other saved; but there is not much of a difference between dying with the body or being held in the darkness of the underworld. Let us look over these things one by one in paragraphs, and discuss them briefly. I considered the eloquence of the sons of man, whom God chose. Only this eloquence, he says, God wanted to be between men and beasts, since we speak, they are mute; we possess the will for conversation, they are stupefied with silence. And though we only differ from beasts in language, though it is shown to us, how we are like the beasts - weak in body. Just as a beast dies, thus man dies, and one breath is for all, and that is the air that we breathe. For he says this: "and one spirit is for both, and there is nothing more for man than for beast." Since lest we think the text refers to the soul he adds: "all are made from earth and return to the earth." But nothing else except the body is made from earth, and quite relevant, regarding the body he continues: "you are earth and to the earth you will return."[34] But this seems to be blasphemy: for who knows if the spirit of the sons of man ascends upwards, or if the

31

spirit of beasts goes downwards into the earth? He does not contend that there is no difference between animals and men in reference to the dignity of the soul, but in adding "who?" he wants to show the difficulty of the matter. For the pronoun "who" is used in the Holy Scriptures not on account of impossibility, but a difficulty. So here it is said in that passage, "who will describe that man's generation?"[35], and in the psalm: "Lord, who ascends in your tabernacle, and onto your sacred mountain?"[36], and other examples that follow this pattern. And in Jeremiah it can be said differently in Hebrew: "And he is a man, and who knows him?"[37]. This then, is the only difference between beast and men, that the spirit of man ascends to the heaven, and the spirit of the beast descends into the earth and is dispersed with the flesh; but let any man, who is of the Church and learned in the religious disciplines, be the real champion of the matter, which is rather doubtful. Then he adds just how much it refers to a spiritual understanding: "since the Lord will keep both men and beasts safe"[38], and in another place he says, "beasts, I am among you"[39], and all the prophets say that both men and beasts will be saved in Jerusalem, and that the promised land will be filled with sheep and cattle. Who knows whether the saintly man, who is worthy of the name of man, will ascend to heaven, and whether the sinner, who is called beast, will go down into the earth? For it is possible in light of the uncertain and dangerous condition of his life, that the righteous man falls and the sinner rises, and it sometimes happens that man, having more reason and learned in the Scriptures, does not look about himself, and although worthy of his knowledge lives out his life and is led down to the nether world; and the simpler and unlearned man, who is said to be compared to the beasts of men, lives better and is crowned in martyrdom, and he is then to live in paradise.

3:22. I *therefore observed that there is nothing better for man than to be happy in what he is doing, for that is his lot. For who can enable him to see what will be after him?* Instead of that which we have as "to see what will be after him", Symmachus interprets it more clearly saying, "so that he sees those things which will be after these ones". Therefore nothing is good in life, unless a man is happy in his work, doing acts of sympathy, and obtaining his future reward in the realm of heaven. We have this one lot, which nor neither thief nor robber values, nor any tyrant has the power to take away, and which follows us after our death. And we will not be able to enjoy our toil again when this life will be over, or know what things will

35 Is. 53, 8.

36 Ps. 14, 1.

37 Ier. 17, 9.

38 Ps. 35, 17.

39 Ps. 72, 23.

be afterwards in the world. Another explanation of this is: I am disturbed by the wickedness of what I have said above, that I think there is no difference between men and beasts, and I have been led into this opinion by wrong conclusions, so that I said nothing else was good, except grasping ones present desire. Nor when death has destroyed us is it possible to enjoy these things, which we, ungrateful, leave behind. Some have referred to that understanding because it says, "for who leads him, so that he sees those things, which will be after him", so that they say, "it is better for a man to enjoy his work" because it is only this that he is able to take away with him from his possessions. For when death comes he will not know what kind of heir he will die with, whether worthy or unworthy, who will enjoy his wealth.

Chapter 4

4:1. And *I returned and contemplated all the acts of oppression that are committed beneath the sun: Behold! Tears of the oppressed with none to comfort them, and their oppressors have the power - with none to comfort them.* After considering this I turned my eyes and attention to this, so that I saw the slanderers and those sustaining chicanery. And look on those who, oppressed unjustly by more powerful men, are not able to find a comforter for their tears. For this is only permitted in disasters and in protest at the ill will of the matter. And wherever there is more distress and inconsolable suffering they see the slanderers as stronger in their difficulties. And this is the cause: because they are not worthy of consolation. He describes this idea more fully in the seventy-second psalm of David, and Jeremiah in his own book.

4:2/3. *So I consider more fortunate the dead, who have already died, than the living, who are still alive. But better than either of them is he who has not yet been, and has never witnessed the evil that is committed under the sun.* In comparison with the difficulties, which trouble mortal men in this world, I had judged the dead to be happier than the living according to that which Job says in his argument regarding the dead: " there they rested with tired bodies, with those who had been in chains, now without cares, not hearing the voice of the expeller."[1] But it is better for these two, for the living it seems and for the deceased, who has not yet been born. For one man will suffer ill, another unclothed will escape it as if from a shipwreck. Moreover he who has not yet been born is happier in that, because he has not yet experienced the ill of the world. But he says this, not because he who has not yet been born, exists before he has been born, and he is happier in this, since he has not yet been weighed down by his body; but better to be sure is not existing, or not having a sense of wealth, than either being unhappy or living unhappily. Just as the Lord speaks to Judas, referring to his coming anguish: "it was better for that man never to have been born"[2], since it would have been better for sure for him not to have existed, than to suffer eternal torture. Some people in fact understand this passage in this way: they say they are better, who have died, than those who are living, it is permitted to them before they were sinners[3]. For until now the living were in battle and were held back as if closed in by the prison of the body; but those who have opposed death are already without cares and have stopped sinning. Just like John, in which he was not greater in respect to the

1 Iob. 3, 17, 18.

2 Matth. 26, 24.

3 Cfr. Origines peri Archon I. 5,5 ; Hier. Epist 124, 3. sqq

34

4 Rom. 7, 14.

sons of women, he is less than him, who is the lowest in the realm of heaven and is freed from the burden of the body. He does not know how to say like the apostle: "I am a wretched man, who will free me from the body of this death?"[4]. But he says he is better than those two, who has not yet been born, nor does not see the wickedness, by which men are oppressed in the world. For our souls mingle among the gods, before descending to these bodies and are blessed so long as the heavenly ones are held in Jerusalem and in the choir of angels.

4:4. And *I saw that all labour and skilful enterprise spring from man's rivalry with his neighbour. This, too, is futility and a vexation of the spirit!* I turned my attention once again to other things and I saw the strength and honour of those men who were toiling, and I discovered the good of one man to be the evil of another, while the envious one is tortured by another's happiness, and the boastful lies open to trickery. For what is more vain, what is for nothing like the spirit in this way, than for man to weep for misfortunes that are not his own, or to bemoan his own sins, or be envious of better men.

5 Cfr Prov. 19, 24.

4:5. The *fool folds his hands and eats his own flesh.* This is the man that is described as slow to comprehend in Proverbs[5], holding his chest in his hands. For poverty, although he is a fast runner, catches up with him and he eats his own flesh because of the extent of his hunger, but this is said in exaggeration. He is the sort of man who thinks that having one fist of corn and living idly and in a stupor is better than filling each hand by working. But he sows everything so that he can show that he that both works and acquires possessions leaves himself open in the world to envy. Conversely he that desires to live a simple life is oppressed by poverty and because of this both of these two is poor: while the one runs a risk on account of his wealth, the other is consumed by want because of his poverty. Or indeed perhaps it is to be understood in this way: he who envies the happiness of another man is seized as if by the fury of the spirit, and takes envy into his lap, and nourishes it in his heart: thus it is he eats his soul and his flesh. For as much as he sees that man whom he envies as happier, he himself more so wastes away and perishes, and little by little becomes more full of envy and jealousy. Another way of reading this is: his hands are taken on many occasions to lead him to work, just as the passage which states, "the act of the Lord which

35

is done in the hand of Haggai"[6], or of Ecclesiastes, or of his prophet, because he has done such work, that he appears to be worthy, in whose work is the speech of the Lord. And the man, who corresponds to this man is David, "who leads my hands in battle"[7]. Therefore the fool embraces his hands, that is he draws them together and doesn't want to open them, and so does not eat the toil of his hands, which he does not have, but his flesh, living by the wisdom of his flesh and eating the toil of his flesh.

4:6. *Better is one handful of pleasantness than two fistfuls of labour and vexation of the spirit.* It is better to have modest power, than great riches of sins. And in Proverbs it says, "To receive a little through righteousness is better than gaining much by injustice." [8] Justice rightly has rest, injustice toil. And since a single number is always seen in a good context and a dual seen as wickedness, therefore one fist has rest, and two hands are full of toil.

4:7/8. *Then I returned and contemplated futility beneath the sun: a lone and solitary man who has neither son nor brother, yet there is no end to his toil, nor is his eye ever sated with riches, nor does he ask himself, 'For whom am I toiling and depriving myself of goodness.' This too is futility, indeed, it is a sorry task.* I turned to other people and I saw that they work more than is necessary and amass wealth by good and bad means and do not use it once accumulated; they have all things, brood over their riches, keep it for another, and do not enjoy their work. Then at the end of their life they have neither son nor brother, nor close friend so that the pious work seems reserved for necessities only. And so I discovered nothing more vain than that man, who collects riches, or to whom an ignorant man bequeaths them. We are even able to understand this in a religious interpretation, and understand it as those, who write books and leave them to fastidious readers. Some say that this passage from where it says "there is one, but there is not a second" is about the Saviour, because he came down to save the world alone and without any companion. And although there are many sons of God, they are called his brothers by adoption, though not one remains worthy, who should be joined to him in this work. There is no end to this work, for those carrying our faults and sins and suffering for us; and his eye will not be filled by riches, but always with those desiring our safety, and the more you see his sins, the more he encourages him to repent.

6 Hagg. 1, 1.

7 Ps. 143, 1.

8 Prov. 16, 8.

4:9/12. *Two are better than one, for they get a greater return for their labour. For should they fall, one can raise the other; but woe to him who is alone when he falls and there is no one to raise him! Also, if two sleep together they keep warm, but how can one be warm alone? Where one can be overpowered, two can resist attack; A three-ply cord is not easily severed!* After the misfortunes of loneliness in which he has been seized, and he who torments himself in acquiring wealth without a definite heir, now the subject of companionship is treated. And it asks what good ther is in a tent of friends and what comfort there is in company, since one man's distress or domestic strife is lifted by another's help, (any man who has a faithful friend will sleep better all that night, than he who sleeps only with his wealth which he has amassed. And if a stronger enemy rises up against one man, the weakness of one is sustained by the comfort of friends. And just as two differ from one if they are joined in love, so the tent of three is stronger. For even true charity, which has been violated by no envy increases as much in number as it grows in strength. And this idea is conveyed in relatively few words. But since previously we have placed the discussion of the intelligence of certain men before Christ, those things which are still left must be discussed by the same order. It is better for two to be equal, than one. For it is better for a man who lives alone to have Christ, than alone to leave himself vulnerable to ill-intentioned plots. Since the reward of the tent is shown at once in the very usefulness of society. For if one man fell, Christ would raise up his partner. Woe indeed to him who collapses, he will not have Christ rising up in him. For if one sleeps, that is, if he had been dissolved by death and had Christ with him, he will revive more quickly having been made warm and given life once again. And if the devil, being stronger in his attack, should attack a man, the man will stand, and Christ will stand in place of this man, in place of his companion. Not because virtue is weak (the virtue of Christ alone) against the devil, but because the decision of man is left free and for us, who are dependent, but virtue itself will become stronger through fighting. And even if the Father, and the Son, and the Holy Spirit should come, that friendship is not broken easily. But although it is not broken easily, it will be broken nonetheless at some point. And the cord from the apostle to Judas was threefold: but after the breaking of the bread Satan entered him and that cord was broken. More precisely what he says above is, "and even if two are sleeping, then they will be warm: and how will one keep warm on his own?" We can take an example from Elisha, because he is in a pact with a lad, and slept with him and warmed his body, and in

37

9 Cfr IV Reg. 4, 32-36.

this way revived the recovering boy.[9] Unless therefore Christ sleeps with us and rests in death, we are not able to receive the heart of eternal life.

4:13/16. *Better is a poor but wise youth, than an old and foolish king who no longer knows how to take care of himself; because from the prison-house he emerged to reign, while even in his reign he was born poor. I saw all the living that wander beneath the sun throng to the succeeding youth that steps into his place. There is no end to the entire nation, to all that was before them; similarly the ones that come later will not rejoice in him. For this too is futility and a vexation of the spirit.* Symmachus translates this passage in this way: "better a poor man who has wisdom, than an old and foolish king who does not know to beware of change". For the one leaves the body to reign in heaven, and the other indeed, although he had been born a king, is restricted by poverty. I saw all men living, who grow up under the sun in propitious adolescence, which increases in them. Each and every nation that was before is unending, and those that come after do not rejoice in the previous. But this too is empty and a vexation of the spirit. My Hebrew tutor, whose teachings I often refer to, bore witness while he was reading Ecclesiastes with me, that Bar Akiba wrote these things above the present passage, and he is greatly admired by other scholars: better is the inner part of man, which arises in us after the fourteenth year of puberty, than the outer, physical man, who is born from his mother's womb, and he does not know how to abstain from vice because it comes to this that he rules over his vices from the house of chains, that is from his mother's womb. For he is made poor because of his power and by carrying out all wicked deeds. I saw those men, who lived as those former men, and were changed afterwards into that second man, in him that has been born in place of the former. And I understood that all men sinned in that prior manhood, before the second is born, when they become two men. But once these men have changed for the better, and after the learning of philosophers, they leave the left path and hurry towards the right, and they follow the second man, that is the newest man, and do not rejoice in him that is the former. The apostle agrees with these two types of men[10] and Leviticus also mentioned them: "Man, man"[11] who desired this or that. That saintly man Gregorius Pontus the bishop, to whom Origen preached, understands the passage in the following way in his *Metaphrasis of Ecclesiastes:* "I however prefer a youth who is poor yet is growing wise, to an old king who is foolish, to whom it never occurs that it is possible for

10 Cfr Rom, 7, 15.

11 Cfr Lev. 17, 13; 19, 20; 21, 17. etc.

someone from those whom he has conquered, will leave the body to reign in heaven; and then he destroys himself from his unjust power. For it happens though that those who were growing wise at the time of youth are without sadness; but that they changed before the time of becoming an old king. For those that have been born afterwards, since they do not know the wickedness that has gone before, they are not able to praise youth, which arises afterwards, and are led astray by perverse ideas and by the force of the opposing arguments."[12] Laodicenus has asserted that great matters are expressed in this short passage, and he wrote here in his accustomed fashion: "Ecclesiastes now speaks about the change of good men into wicked, expressing the foolish man as he who tries, and who not thinking of the future, enjoys the transient and failing things as if they are great and perpetual. And after the many things which usually happen (or change) to men in their life, he asserts something of a general opinion of death, since the great number perishes and little by little is consumed and pass across, with each one leaving the other in his place, and another's successor dying."[13] Origines and Victorinus[14] did not think very differently on this matter. After the general statement that reveals to all that the poor yet wise youth is better than an old king who is foolish, and that it often happens that the lad leaves the prison of the king because of his wisdom, and commands in place of a cruel dictator, and as a foolish king loses all his power, which he had obtained. They saw this passage in relation to Christ and the devil, because they wished to view the poor and wise boy as Christ. The poor boy is the same as that one in "it is great for you to be called my boy"[15], but the poor man, since he has been made poor[16], when once he was rich and wise, because "he was proficient in age and wisdom and thankful to God and men."[17] That man is born in the reign of an old man and therefore he says, "if this was my rule in the world, that my servants struggle on my behalf so that I am not handed over to the Jews. But now it is not my rule."[18] So in the reign of that foolish old man who displays all the rule of the whole world and his glory, the most excellent boy comes from the house of chains, about which Jeremiah speaks in Lamentations, saying, "so that he lowers to the feet of that man all those who have been conquered in the world."[19] And that boy goes on to rule and goes away to a far off region, and as king after some time is turned against those, who do not want to rule. So with some insight Ecclesiastes saw that all men who are alive and who are able to be part of youth, say, "I am life"[20], having left behind them that old foolish king, to follow Christ. At the same time the two nations of Israel are to be understood here. The first,

12 Grego. Neocaesar. Metaphr. In Eccl. -PG 10, 1000 A

13 Apollinarius Laodic.

14 Origenes. Victorinus Poetouion

15 Is. 49, 6. According to LXX

16 cfr II Cor. 8, 9.

17 Luc. 2, 52.

18 Ioh. 18, 36.

19 Thren. 3, 34.

20 Ioh. 14, 6.

which was before the arrival of the Lord, and the next, which will support the Antichrist in place of Christ, for the first is not deep down despondent, since the first church was formed from Jews and the apostles; and in the end the Jews, who will support the Antichrist, will not rejoice in Christ.

4:17. *Guard your foot when you go to the House of God; better to draw near and hearken than to offer the sacrifices of fools, for they do not consider that they do evil.* He gives some general precepts for life, and does not want to offend us, who go to church. Since it is praiseworthy in his view, not just to enter the House of God, but to enter without offence. And if it was intended for all who are in the church of God to hear this passage, he would never have added, "and approach so that you might hear". But then it was only Moses who approached near to God to hear[21], the other men were not allowed. For the foolish commit sins, not knowing that there is a remedy; they think that they can satisfy God with the offering of gifts, and do not know that this is also evil and a sin; for they want to make correction for what they have done, not with obedience and good work, but with gifts and sacrifice. What others have said elsewhere agrees with this too: "obedience above sacrifice"[22]. And "I want pity and not sacrifice".[23]

21 Cfr Ex. 24, 2

22 I Reg. 15, 21.

23 Os. 6, 6

40

Chapter 5

5:1/2. *Be not rash with your mouth, and let not your heart be hasty to utter a word before God; for God is in heaven and you are on earth, so let your words be few. For a dream comes from much concern, and foolish talk from many words.* Several men think that this teaches here that we should not promise something too quickly in the presence of God, and without due consideration of our strengths we vow things, which we cannot then fulfil. God though is present in heaven, but we seem to be on earth, yet he hears what we say and accuses that our foolishness comes from our love of speech. But some men understand this better, affirming that this teaches that, either speaking or thinking more about God than we are able, we hold to our opinions; but we know our stupidity, since, as much as the heavens differ from the earth, so our thoughts are separated from His character. And therefore our words ought to be checked. Just as he that is much in thought frequently dreams about those things about which he thinks during the day; thus he, who wanted to teach more from divinity, falls into foolishness. Or indeed it could mean this: our words ought to be few therefore, since even those things, which we think we know, we see through a mirror and in mystery, and as we understand a dream, which we think we can grasp. Although we have done many things, as it appears to us, the end of our argument is foolishness. For we do not escape sin by too much speaking[1].

1 Cfr Prov. 10, 19.

5:3/4. *When you make a vow to God, do not delay paying it, for He has no liking for fools; what you vow, pay. Better that you not vow at all, than that you vow and not pay.* A simple man does not need understanding by interpretation. It is better not to promise than not to keep promises, since they displease God and are numbered among fools, who do not fulfil their vows. But since he says, "There is no will in fools" underneath we hear "of God", like the word of the apostle, who says, "and just as there was no will, that I should now come to you"[2]. For even if we want to say something more inquiring, it is taught to a Christian, that he should fulfil his faith by work, and not be like the Jews, who pledge and say, "we will do all that God commands"[3], and yet worship idols. And afterwards they beat those slaves and cast stones at them, and immediately killed the very son of the father of their house. It is better therefore to hold a doubtful opinion for a while, which is easy

2 I Cor. 16, 12.

3 Ex. 24, 3.

to say in words, but difficult to put into practice. For the slave, who knows the will of his God and will not do it will be defeated by many.

5:5. Let *not your mouth bring guilt on your flesh, and do not tell the messenger that it was an error. Why should God be angered by your speech and destroy the work of your hands?* What the Hebrew means is that if you are not able to do these things, do not promise to do them. For the words do not transgress to the spirit but are carried at once to the Lord by the angel present, who sticks to one man only as a companion. You who think to disregard God, since you have promised, you will anger Him, with the result that all your work will be destroyed. But in that place where he says: "to bring guilt upon your flesh" and he understood this, though not caring diligently, as if he had said "let not your mouth cause you not to sin." But there seems to me however another meaning, which is argued by those, who complain about the strength of the flesh and say they are compelled by the necessity of the body to do those things that they don't want to do, according to the apostle: "for I do not do what I want, but what I do not wish" and so on.[4] And so he says, 'don't seek vain excuses and give occasion to your flesh to sin'. Then in that place where he says "and do not tell the angel that it was a madness" Aquila takes the Hebrew word *segaga* to mean ignorance, and translates it with the Greek word *akousion*, that is, not of ones will. For if you say this, he says, you provoke God, as if to say He is like the creator of evil and sin, and anger Him, so that if you seem to have anything good, He will take it from your possession. Or indeed he translates such things with the meaning of reproof, so that you do those things, which are not appropriate.

5:6. *In spite of all dreams, futility and idle chatter, rather: Fear God!* The Hebrews explain this passage in great detail, and in the following way: and you should not do the things detailed above, about which he has already spoken, lest you believe too readily in dreams. For when you see different things, your mind will be troubled by many fears throughout your night's rest, or aroused by promises, you despise those things that are dream-like. You should only fear God. For he, who believes in dreams, gives himself over to vanities and nonsense. Another meaning of this passage is, since I have said and admonished, "you should not let your mouth bring guilt on your flesh", and to seek this or that excuse; I introduce this now, since in the dream of that life, and in the appearance, shade, cloud in which we live, we are able to find many things, which seem

4 Rom. 7, 15

42

true to life to us and excuse our sins. Therefore I advise that you beware that alone, lest you think God is absent, but fear Him, and know He is present in all your toil, and do not force yourself to be hidden in free will, but want whatever it is that you do.

5:7/8. *If you see oppression of the poor, and the suppression of justice and right of the State, do not be astonished at the fact, for there is One higher than the high Who watches and there are high ones above them. The advantage of land is supreme; even a king is indebted to the soil.* Christ's garment, woven on top, was not able to be torn by those who crucified him; and the Saviour threw him from that demon, and advised him to go away having put on the clothes of the apostles. So we believe that the clothes of our Ecclesiastes are not to be torn, nor should we sew on here and there patches in place of our free-will of opinion, but use the one text itself in dispute, and follow the same meaning and arrangement all the way through. Above this he had said: "do not tell the messenger that it was a madness, lest God become angry over your speech", and regarding the remaining things, he had spoken against those, who do not know that providence rules over human affairs. Since therefore the question arises many times about the precept, why the righteous sustain disaster, and why the unjust become judges over all the world, but God is not vengeful: now he introduces and finishes this argument, saying, 'if you see the calamity of a pauper, who is said to be blessed in the Gospel, and the situation is assessed according to his strength and not in justice, do not be astonished or let anything seem new to you. God, who is highest above the high, sees these things, He that placed His angels above the judges and kings of the earth, to prevent injustice and they are more important on earth, than any of man's potentates. But since he will be the Saviour at the end of the judges, and in the end of the world when the cornfield will be ripe, and the harvesters will come, he will be ordered that the wheat be separated and the darnel thrown on the fire. Therefore he now awaits and differs in opinion, although the field of the world is cultivated carefully more fully. But since that field is interpreted as the world, the Lord expounds about them in the parable of darnel and wheat.[5]

5 Cfr Matth. 13, 24-30.

5:9/10. *A lover of money will never be satisfied with money; a lover of abundance has no wheat. This too, is futility! As goods increase, so do those who consume them; what advantage, then, has the owner except what hi eyes see?* Wherever we read 'silver',

43

according to the ambiguity of the Greek term, it can be translated as 'money', since each has the meaning of the Greek *argurion*. More precisely Tullius is said to have called these men 'pecuniary', who have many small savings, that is wealth in cattle.[6] For they were called this in antiquity. But little by little the word devolved into the one used here through misuse. Therefore he is described as greedy because he is never sated by wealth, and the more he has, the more he desires. Horace also agrees with this sentiment, who says, "always the miser is wanting"[7], and too the noble historian, since "avarice is diminished neither by possessions, nor by lack of them". Nothing therefore, says Ecclesiastes can aid a man who possesses riches, unless only this: that he sees what he possesses. For the greater his wealth, the more he will have a larger number of servants, who use up his amassed wealth. But if he will only see what he has, he will be able to take more than the food of one man.

6 (because the Latin for cattle is pecus)

7 Horat. Epist. I. 2, 56.

5:11. Sweet *is the sleep of the labourer, whether he eats little or much; the satiety of the rich does not let him sleep.* So far the discourse has treated of riches and greed, and it is compared to a man who works and one who sleeps without worry, or eats little or a great deal. Because he eats any food obtained from the toil of work and from his sweat, he enjoys peaceful sleep. For a rich man indeed is busy with banquets and lacerated by many thoughts, is not able to sleep, and abounds in hangovers and uncooked food boils in the intestines of his stomach. More precisely, since it is called sleep, and is a common exit from life, that rest will be better for him, who is busy at present and reserves his strength for good work, than the riches of those men, about whom it is written: "woe to you, O rich, for you have received your consolation".[9]

9 Sallust Cati. 11.3

5:12/16. *There is a sickening evil that I have seen under the sun; riches hoarded by their owner to his misfortune, and he loses those riches in some bad venture. If he begets a son, he has nothing in hand. As he had come from his mother's womb, naked will he return, as he had come; he can salvage nothing from his labour to take with him. This too, is a sickening evil: Exactly as he came he must depart, and what did he gain in exchange for toiling for the wind? Indeed, all his life he eats in darkness; he is greatly grieved, and has illness and anger.* Take what follows as linked to what is written above: while Ecclesiastes describes wealth, even he is not

44

able to enjoy his riches and on many occasions endangers himself on account of them. Nor to his heir does he leave what he has amassed; but even he and his son, just as they came nude, will return nude to the earth and nothing of their toil will accompany them. Surely apathy is the worst, to be tortured by thought on account of riches, and wealth will perish. And are we able to take it with us when we die, in sadness, in mourning, in indignation, in laws or to seek it in vain toil? And all this is according to the apparent simple meaning of the text. But as we are lifted higher, it seems to me that it speaks about the philosophers, or the heretics, who amass riches of doctrines into their wickedness, and nor are authors able to follow any usefulness, nor leave perpetual fruit for their followers. But even they and their disciples return to the earth and lose their riches, from him who said, "I will lose the wisdom of the wise men, and I will reprove the prudence of the careful."[10] Truly in fact, just as they left their mother's womb, (apparently as from a heretical church), contrary to this about which it is written: "but Jerusalem which is above is free, which is the mother of all."[11] Thus they go nude to become a spirit, and work for nothing. Those who examine, lack examination, and they are carried on every wind of doctrine, nor do they have the light, but eat their sacraments in the darkness. They are always ill, and are easily moved to anger, storing up anger for themselves for the day of anger, and they do not have the favour of God.

10 I Cor. 1, 19.

11 Gal. 4, 26.

5:17/19 *So what I have seen to be good is that it is suitable to eat and drink and enjoy pleasure with all one's labour that he toils beneath the sun during the brief span of his life that God has given him, for that is his lot. Furthermore, every man to whom God has given riches and possessions and has given him the power to enjoy them, possess his share and be happy in his work: this is the gift of God. For he shall remember that the days of his life are not many, while God provides him with the joy of his heart.* This is in comparison to him, who consumes his wealth in the darkness of his worries, and carries those things which are about to die throughout the great tedium of his life, and says that that man is better, who enjoys what he has. For here there is but a small desire of enjoyment, but there in the latter indeed there is a great magnitude of worries. He also gives the reasons why the gift of God is to be able to enjoy riches. Since "he will not remember much of the days of his life". For God turns him to the happiness of his heart's desire: he

12 Cf I Cor. 10, 2-4.

will not be sad, he will not be worried by thought, since he is led away by happiness and desire for present things. But it is better understood as according to the apostle[12], seen as spiritual food and spiritual drink which is given by God and I understood to see goodness in all of his toil, since we are only able to consider true good things with great toil and enthusiasm. For what is permitted to be good, though, until Christ appears in our life, is not yet openly considered good. And therefore God will not remember much of the days of our life. We should also note that here *perispasmos* is used in a better way, in the place of the occupation of the spirit and true happiness.

Chapter 6

6:1/6. *There is an evil I have observed beneath the sun, and it is prevalent among mankind; a man to whom God has given riches, wealth and honour, and he lacks nothing that his heart could desire, yet God did not give him the power to enjoy it. This is futility and an evil disease. If a man begets an hundred children and lives many years - great being the days of his life - and his soul is not content with the good - and he even is deprived of burial; I say: the stillborn is better off than he. Though its coming is futile and it departs in darkness, though its very name is enveloped in darkness, though it never saw the sun nor knew; it has more satisfaction than he. Even if he should live a thousand years twice over, but find no contentment - do not all go to the same place?* He describes the riches of misers and asserts that this evil is often in men, since none of those things, which are thought to be good in the world, is lacking in him, and nonetheless he torments himself with the most inane sparing, saving those things to be devoured by others. Nor does he say this in exaggeration, for even if he produced an hundred books and lived longer than Adam, that is almost one thousand years, but lived two thousand years, he would rot his mind with desire and avarice. He is born prematurely in a worse state that dies, as soon as he seems born. For he did not see evil things or good things; but although he used to possess good things, he was tormented by thoughts and sadness, and having been born prematurely he has more rest, than a greedy man who is old. But both however are seized by the same fate, while both the first and the last are taken away by the same death. This could also refer to Israel, because God gave Israel the law, which speaks about the prophets, the testament, the Promised Land and the Saviour: "let the reign of God be removed from you and given to a nation that brings forth his fruit"[1]. All these things have been given to a foreign and pilgrim people from peoples who see their good yet do not enjoy it. They say we are of much better condition, who are considered to be as new-born and premature by those, who praised themselves in antiquity, finding glory in their fathers, saying: "our father was Abraham"[2], but however both we and they hasten to one place, that is to the judgement of God. But what Ecclesiastes says in the

1 Matth. 21, 43.

2 Ioh. 8, 39

47

middle is this: "but there was no tomb for him". This either means that that rich man does not think of his death, and while he possesses all, is greedy even in building a tomb; or that often he is killed on account of those riches, by plots against his life, and is left unburied, or, what I think is a better interpretation, he needs nothing of good deeds, from which he is able to obtain for himself memory among those who come after him. And so that he will not pass through life in silence, just as cattle, although he had a means, by which he was able to show that he had lived.

6:7/8. *All man's toil is for his mouth, yet his wants are never satisfied. What advantage then has the wise man over the fool? What less has the pauper who knows how to conduct himself among the living?* All that men toil at in this world is consumed by the mouth and taken to be digested in the stomach after it has been ground down by the teeth. And when a little bit has pleased the palette, it seems to create a desire, so long as it is held in the mouth. But when it has passed down to the stomach the difference between foods is no longer distinguishable. And after all these things the spirit of a man who eats is not filled up; or then he desires again what he has eaten, and is as wise as the fool without food, who does not know how to live, and the poor man asks for nothing else but for how he is to sustain the organs of his meagre body, and not die through starvation. Or because the spirit takes no gain from the food of the body, and food is of equal use to a wise man and a fool, and the pauper wanders therefrom, to where he has seen wealth to be. This is better understood regarding a man of the church, who learned in the heavenly Scriptures, holds all his toil in his mouth yet his spirit is not filled, for he always desires to learn. And in that respect the wise man has more than the fool, since when he feels himself to be poor, he presses that pauper, who is called blessed in the Gospel, to understand those things which are of life, and walks the restricted and narrow path, which leads to life, and he is poor from wicked deeds and knows where Christ, (who is life) is to be found.

6:9. Better *is what the eyes see than what is imagined. That, too, is futility and a vexation of the spirit.* Symmachus interpreted this clearly, he says: "it is better to make provision, than to walk about as it pleases you". That is, it is better to do all things according to what you know to be right in your mind, which is the eye of the soul, than to follow the desire of your heart. For this is to wander in

48

spirit, just as Ezekiel says: "he who walks by the desire of his heart"[3]. For indeed he denounced that man is proud and only pleases himself and says he is better, who makes provision for all days, than he, whom nothing pleases, unless he has made it himself. Nothing is worse than him, and more vane than any breath. And again here "vexation of the spirit" has been interpreted by Theodotion and Aquila as 'suffering of the soul'. Symmachus too has "affliction of the spirit". More precisely we must remember that in Hebrew 'spirit' and 'breath' are similar in usage - that is *ruha*.

3 Ezek. 11, 21.

6:10. *What has been was already named, and it is known that he is but a man. He cannot contend with one who is mightier than him.* Clearly this is predicting the arrival of the Saviour, since he writes 'he will be'; before he was seen in body his name was already written in the Scriptures and was known by prophets and holy men of God, since he was a man; and similar to this, since he is a man, he is not able to walk with his Father. And in the Gospel it says: "the Father, who sent me, is greater than me."[4] In the following passages it teaches not to ask more than is written for us by Him, so that a man may not wish to know more than is attested in the Scriptures. For although we are ignorant of our condition and our life passes us by like a shadow, and our future is undecided, it is not useful for us to strive for more than we are able to attain. Some think that this passage means that God already knows the names of all the men, who will be in the future, and who will be enclosed within the body of mankind. Nor is a man able to reply to his creator, and ask why he has been made in this way or that. For however much more we seek, our vanity and our unnecessary words are exposed all the more. Our choice does not come free from the foreknowledge of God, but precedes the causes, why any one thing is done in a particular way.

4 Ioh. 14, 28.

6:11. *There are many things that increase futility;*

Chapter 7

7:1. [+6:12.] *How does it benefit man? For who knows what is good for man in this life, all the days of his vain life, which he spends as a shadow? For who can tell a man what will be after him under the sun?* When he says that man is ignorant of his condition, and does not actually know whatever he seems to know and discern, as if the truth of the matter is not seen, he does see however the shadow and image as if through a mirror, and he cannot know what will come, or escape his sin by talkativeness. He should silence his mouth and believe that He who is written has come, and not ask by what means, how much, or what kind of man he is that has come.

7:2. [KJV. 7:1. sic seq.] *A good name is better than precious ointment; and the day of death than the day of one's birth.* Consider, he says, man, your short days since you will cease to be quickly when your body gives out; fast longer, so that however perfume delights your nostrils with its smell, in the same way posterity will delight in all things to your name. Symmachus interpreted this very clearly, saying, "a good name is better than a perfume that smells pleasant". We must remember that it is the custom of the Hebrews to call good perfume 'oil'. He also says, **"and the day of death than the day of one's birth"**, this shows that it is better to die, and no longer be troubled, or be in an unsteady condition of life, than sustain all these things while being born into the world. For in our death we know what we have been like, but when we are born we cannot know what we will be like or do in life. Since birth is also linked to the freedom of the spirit in the body, it abolishes moral customs.

7:3. *It is better to go to the house of mourning, than to go to the house of feasting: for that is the end of all men; and the living will take it to his heart.* It is more useful to go to the rites of a funeral than to the house where there is a party, since at the house of mourning we are warned of our creator and of our mortality on account of seeing the dead body. But in the happiness of a party, even if we seem to have any fear, we lose it. Symmachus interpreted the last verse by saying, "and he who lives, will look back in his mind". There is proof in these verses, in that God is seen to approve food and drink, but not seen to prefer desire to all these things, with the result that many men value them wrongly. But in comparison with avarice and too much sparing, feasting is allowed in a small way, or allowed to him, who enjoys his work completely every moment. For he had never preferred the sadness of mourning to the enjoyment of a party, if he had thought at any moment to drink and eat.

7:4. *Anger is better than laughter, for through a sad face the heart is improved.* Laughter weakens the mind, anger reproves and corrects it. Both let us become angry with ourselves when we sin, and let us get angry with others. Through the sadness of the face, even the spirit becomes better, as Symmachus saw it. And therefore "woe now to those who laugh, since they will mourn."[1]

1 Luc. 6, 25.

2 Matth. 5, 5.

3 Cfr I Reg. 1(

4 Cfr II Cor. 1
21.

7:5. *The heart of the wise is in the house of mourning; but the heart of fools is in the house of enjoyment.* "Blessed", says the Saviour, "are the mourning, since they will be consoled".[2] And Samuel mourned King Saul all the days of his life[3] and Paul said he had mourned over those who did not want to repent their many sins[4]. Therefore the heart of a wise man goes to the house of such a man, who reproves himself when he is doing wrong, so that he brings forth tears and causes himself to weep for his own sins; and he does not go to the house of joy, where the learned man flatters and deceives, not changing the listeners so they are together as one, but asking for praise and applause from them. Such a teacher, who is rich in speeches and words, is mourned, and being filled by his knowledge, receives his consolation. Then the following verses agree with this explanation too, because he says:

7:6/7. *It is better to hear the rebuke of the wise, than for a man to hear the song of fools. For as the crackling of thorns under the pot, so is the laughter of the fool: this too is vanity.* For it is better to be rebuked by a wise man, than to be deceived by flattering praise. Similar to this is the passage which says, "better are the wounds of a friend, than the free kisses of an enemy"[5]. Just as the sound of sharp thorns under the pot gives out a harsh sound, so the words of a flattering teacher are not of any use, or the worries of the world, which are interpreted as 'thorns', or the sound of one who encourages his listeners, or of one who prepares them for the fire which is to come. Let us look at what Symmachus has to say about the passage that we have as "since just as the sound…fool." Understanding the meaning which we have already explained above, he says, 'for a man is bound in chains by the voice of the ignorant". This means that one listener is tied up to the word of such teachers, while the chains of his sins restrain another.

5 Prov. 27, 6.

51

6 Prov. 9, 8.

7 Deut. 16, 19

7:8. *Surely oppression makes a wise man mad; and a gift destroys the heart.* Now see the wise man as if regarding profit, according to that passage which says, "accuse the wise and he will love you"[6]. Wise, or even having completed his training, he knows no accusation, and is perturbed by no disaster. We should use this verse if we see disaster befall a righteous and wise man, and he is perturbed by the unlawfulness of the judgement, and in that case when God does not come to his mind readily. Instead of this though the Septuagint, and Aquila and Theodotion interpret the phrase "destroys the heart" as *eutonias autou* that is 'his strength', or 'his vigour'. Symmachus says, "and *matthana* destroys his heart' (that is 'a gift'), using the Hebrew word in his interpretation, and making the same meaning as is written elsewhere: "gifts, too, blind the eyes of the wise".[7]

7:9. Better *is the end of a thing than the beginning;* Perorations are better in speaking, than just the introductory section. For worry comes to and end in the former, and commences in the latter. Or it could even mean this: he who begins to hear a speech, and goes to the teacher, is in first place. For indeed he who listens until the last is consumed and complete in learning. But this can also be understood in this way: while we are in this world, all that we know is as a beginning; but when that age is completed, we will understand everything as newest and completed. My Hebrew tutor explained this passage together with the following verse as follows: it is better for you to ponder the end of your business, than the beginning, and be patient, rather than being seized by the frenzy of impatience. We learn too from this reading that there is no wisdom in men, although it is better to do than to only say that you will do. And since, when the talk had finished, the listener thinks over for himself what has been said, and though he begins to speak, he has not yet understood what he can learn from it.

And the patient in spirit is better than the proud in spirit. Since the heavenly one conceded to anger, saying, "anger is better than laughter", lest we think anger is to be praised in suffering, now he says that anger must be removed from deep down inside us. For there he assigns anger instead of correction in sinners, and learning in children. But here he checks impatience. But patience is not only necessary in difficult times, but also in happier times, in case we rejoice more than we should. It seems to me that he who is now

52

called high in the spirit of the Gospel, is in contrast poor in spirit, and is even blessed.

7:10. Be *not hasty in your spirit to be angry: for anger rests in the lap of fools.* He does not grant here that anger should be tempered, therefore he now says, "Be not hasty in your spirit to be angry"; but that when anger is mad and new, it is more easily tempered because it is dispersed easily and can be removed. And since anger is linked to pride, and the desire for vengeance, he says it is better and above suffering, than he who is exalted in his spirit, and now shows the sign of foolishness, since however powerful or wise someone is esteemed, if he is made angry he will seem foolish in his words: "for anger lies in the lap of fools".

7:11. Do *not ask,' what is the cause that the former days were better than these?' For you do not enquire wisely about this.* Do not prefer the previous age to this one, since God created both one and the other. Virtues create good days for man, and vices make bad days. Do not say therefore that the days were better in the time of Moses and Christ, than now they are. For even in that time there were more disbelievers and their days were made wicked by this; now there are more believers, about whom the Saviour said, "more blessed are they, who did not see or believe"[8]. Or differently: thus you ought to live so that the days that you live in are always better than those passed, lest you begin to decrease little by little, it should then be said to you, "you did run well, who hindered you that you should not have obeyed the truth?"[9]; and again: "you who began in spirit are now consumed by flesh"[10]. Or another meaning of this: do not say that the times of old are better than now, those of Moses better than Christ, that they were more lawful than full of grace. For if you were to ask this, you would do it unwisely, not seeing how much the Gospel differs from the Old Testament.

7:12/13. *Wisdom is good with an inheritance: and by it there is profit to them that see the sun. For wisdom is a defence, and money is a defence: but the advantage of knowledge is, that wisdom gives life to those that have it.* A wise man with riches has more glory than just a wise man alone. For some men need wisdom, some wealth, but he who is both wise and not rich is able to teach what is good, but meanwhile he can't show what is to be sought. Therefore he says, since the protection of wisdom is the protection of money, then just as wisdom protects, so too money also protects. And lest he seem to detract from wisdom, while he adds to it by good fortune, (for it is not in our power to obtain riches, which

8 Ioh. 20, 29.

9 Gal. 5. 7.

10 Gal. 3. 3.

often the unrighteous own in greater quantity), he therefore shows wisdom to be greater, saying "but the advantage of knowledge is, that wisdom gives life to those that have it." In that respect, he says, wisdom is greater than riches, because without any wealth it preserves those who think themselves rich. Certain scholars see this passage in a different way: they say that he places heredity in place of good association, by which we are the heirs of God, and co-heirs of Christ. Therefore Ecclesiastes wants to teach how much of a difference there is between those who merit seeing the sun (of justice), and have wisdom by their good association, and those in contrast, who without wisdom have only enthusiasm for vice and association. Since even David shows this, saying "the intelligent shine out by their speech, as the shining bodies of the sky"[11], or as Theodotion interpreted this, "just as the brightness of the firmament. Indeed those who wrote my speeches are as the stars of the sky". But we ought to take that protection of silver (or money) according to *anagoge*[12] from which talents and coins are collected in the parables of the Gospels[13], just as when we were under the protection of wisdom and under the protection of such money: "the sun does not burn us by day, nor the moon by night".[14] But this can even be said to be true since protection is our life on the earth: "the breath of our nostrils, the anointed Christ our Lord of whom we said: under His shadow we should live among the heathen".[15] All of our protection in this life is like a shade, or like wisdom, or as is said about money, until the day moves on and the shadows move away. Symmachus interprets this more clearly in his usual manner, saying, "just as wisdom protects, so too money protects in a similar fashion". But the following verse openly encourages the enthusiasm for knowledge.

7:14. Consider *the work of God: for who can make that straight, which he has made crooked?* Symmachus translates this passage in this way: "learn the word of God, because no one can correct what He has ruined". That is he supplies from the Holy Scriptures, or from thinking of the elements, to know and understand those things, which are done; but not to ask the causes and reasons why one thing is done in this way, or why it ought to have been done differently from the way in which it has been done. For the sake of this passage, if anyone should ask why God spoke to Moses in this way: "who makes the dumb and the deaf, the seeing and the blind, am I not the Lord God?"[16], and if he should say, why are the blind, the deaf, the mute created in this way, and others similar to these? This passage must be seen in reference to Psalm 17, in which it is said to

11 Dan. 12. 3.

12 See footnote 50.

13 Cfr Matth. 25, 14-23; Luc. 19. 12-25.

14 Ps. 120, 6.

15 Thren. 4, 20.

16 Ex. 4, 11.

54

17 Ps. 17, 26-27.

18 Lev. 26-27

19 Cfr. Lucr. De Rerum Natura VI 962/965; Verg. Ecl. VIII 80.; Hier. Epist. 120,10 -12. CSEL 55, p504,10

20 Cfr Ovid, Meta. I.19-20.

the Lord: "You will be Holy with the holy man, and with the wicked You will err"[17]. And it must be added that the Holy Lord is with him, who is holy; and the wicked are with him, who was previously wicked by his own will. This is similar also to that which is written in Leviticus: "if the wicked came to me I will go to them, wicked in my madness".[18] Even this can explain why God hardened the heart of Pharaoh. For just as one and the same quality of the sun melts wax and dries clay, and on account of each one's constitution, both wax melts and clay dries;[19] so too the one quality of the portents of God in Egypt softened the heart of those who believed, and hardened that of the incredulous, who just as their hardness and impatient heart, began to store up for themselves anger for the day of anger from those portents, which they didn't believe, though yet they saw them happen.

7:15. In *the day of prosperity be joyful, but in the day of adversity consider: God also has set the one over against the other, to the end that man should find nothing after him.* I have heard from a certain man in the Church, who was thought to have a knowledge of the Scriptures, that these verses are to be explained in this way: while you remain in the present world, and while you are able to do good work, work hard so that afterwards you may be without worry in the day of wickedness, that is the day of judgement, when you will see others to be tormented. For just as God made the present world, in which we can obtain for ourselves the benefits of good work; so too he made the future age, in which no opportunity will be given for us to do good work. This man of the Church even seemed to convince those he was preaching to, but to me there seems a different meaning to this, which Symmachus has translated, saying, 'in the good day, be good; but be wary of the day of wickedness'. All the same, God made this world similar to the next, so that man should not be able to find that which he complains against Him. Suffer both the good things, he says, and the bad, as they happen to you in your life. And do not think that there is only the nature of good or bad alone in the world, especially when the world itself consists of opposites: hot and cold, dry and wet, hard and soft, dark and light, bad and good. [20] But God made this ambivalence so that wisdom might have a place, and it is found by choosing good and avoiding bad: man is given free will, lest he argue that he has been made unfeeling, and stupid by God. But God has made man so diverse that man is unable to complain of his manner of being. At the same time this argument is to be taken with

55

the previous verses, in which he says 'who is able to correct what God has done?'.

7:16. I *have seen all things in the days of my vanity: there is a just man, that dies in his righteousness, and there is a wicked man that remains alive in his wickedness.* Similar to this is what the Saviour says in the Gospel: "he who finds his soul will lose it, and he who loses it on account of me, will find it"[21]. The Maccabees are seen to die on account of their justice by the law and justice of God, and martyrs too, who shed their blood for Christ. On the other hand, those who at that time ate the flesh of pigs and sacrificed to idols after the arrival of the Lord, they are seen to live in this world and to live long lives on account of their wickedness. But it is the endurance of God in secret which causes suffering in those who are not holy, so that they havewickedness in their life, and not to visit sinners for their crimes, and it is as if he saves for the sacrifice so that he can give to the former eternal goodness, and to the latter eternal wickedness. The Hebrews suspect the righteous, who die for their righteousness, the sons of Aaron, since while they think they live righteously, they worship a foreign fire. And they say Manasseh was impious and lived a long life on account of his wickedness, for he then lived a long time in a long reign after having been corrected in prison.

7:17. *Do not be too righteous, do not make yourself too wise: why destroy yourself?* If you should see a man who is harsh and wild to the extent of sinning against his brothers, so that he pardons neither the sinner in his speaking, or he who is slow on account of natural slowness, know that this man is more righteous than is good. For when the Saviour teaches, saying "Do not judge, so that you are not judged"[22], and let none be without sin, even if it was not his life at any given day, the judgement of God is not ignorant of the weak state of man. Therefore do not be too righteous, since accursed conduct in the presence of God carries both a great and a minor burden. Philosophers have placed virtues therefore in the middle, and everything which is either too much either above or below, is thought to be at fault.[23] But he also says, "and do not ask too much, lest you become confused", or "lest you be amazed". For he knows that our mind cannot understand complete wisdom, (or that which is to be measured), and he says that we ought to know the wisdom which must be measured in our mortality. Then even Paul asked of him that was able to know more than man, saying, "why does he yet complain? For who has resisted his will?"[24] He

21 Matth. 10. 39

22 Luc. 6, 37.

23 Cfr. Apuleius. Plat. 2, 5.

24 Rom. 9, 19.

56

25 Ibid. 9, 20.

26 Cfr I Reg. 15.

27 Cfr. Matth. 18. 23-34.

replies, "O man, who are you that reply to God?"[25], and so on. If he had heard the causes of the complaint from the apostle, he who is introduced while he is questioning, by chance he would have been stupefied by numbness and would have felt useful gratitude. Since it is a gift according to that same apostle, which is of no use to him that receives it. The command "do not be too righteous"[26] is interpreted by the Hebrew as being about Saul, who felt pity for Agag, whom the Lord had commanded to be killed. But even that servant from the Gospel whom the Lord had pardoned[27], the Lord himself didn't want to pardon the servant, yet he can be used in this verse because he was too righteous.

28 Ezek. 18, 32.

7:18. Do *not be too wicked, and do not be foolish: why should you die before your time?* When God says, "I do not want the death of the dying, only let him return and live"[28], it suffices to have sinned only once. We ought to raise ourselves up after a catastrophe. For just like those who argue about worldly matters, the swallow knows how to protect its young from poppy seeds, and wounded roes seek wild marjoram to cure themselves. Then why are we ignorant that the cure of repentance is proposed for sinners? But he says, "do not delay in an world that is not yours". We know that Chore, Dathan, and Habiron, on account of their uprising against Moses and Aaron, were suddenly eaten up by a gap in the earth, and in emendation of others, many were judged before the day of judgement even in their lifetime.[29] Therefore he says, "do not add sins to sins, lest you cause God to punish you"

29 Cfr. Num. 16.

7:19. It *is good that you should take hold of this, and do not withdraw your hand; for he that fears God shall come forth of them all.* It is good to do good to righteous men, but also being kind to sinners is not wicked. It is good to keep slaves faithful to you, but it is advised to do this only with those who seek your employment. Even he who fears God and copies his maker, who causes rain to fall over both the righteous and the wicked, enjoys doing good to all without distinction. Another meaning of this is, because this life changes daily with many wretched occurrences, as fortunate as unfortunate, the spirit should be prepared for righteousness and should ask for the pity of God, so that whatever happens, he suffers with a free conscience. For he who fears God is neither raised to fortune, nor crushed by misfortune.

7:20/21. *Wisdom strengthens the wise more than ten mighty men which are in the city. For there is not a just man on the earth, that does good and does not sin.* Therefore wisdom strengthens the

57

righteous, and not even the aid of all the citizens of the city can help him, for although someone may be righteous, yet while he is alive he is subject to vices and sins, and he therefore needs greater protection. Another reading of this is: the ten who hold power and are in the city are angels, who have arrived at the complete number of 'denarii' and are here to help mankind. But if anyone should consider different types of help, the aid of wisdom is better, because that is the aid of our Lord Jesus Christ. For after the angels said, "we would have protected Babylon yet it is not now protected, so let us leave it, and let each one of us go out unto his own land"[30]. Then the teacher of doctors himself came down and healed us with a touch of His finger, we who were spattered with blood, and wet with the blood of sinners, we who weigh out all our possessions against healing. But He healed in that city which is in that world, and 'strengthened in wisdom' or as the Septuagint says 'helped'. For it is given and added to everyone who possesses it. But the man who sins greatly is stuck in deep and needs more help: therefore Wisdom herself came to his aid. Another meaning of this verse is: above he had said that one should be kind to both the good and the wicked: therefore someone was able to reply: though I want to be kind to all men, I have not the power with which to do this. And a righteous man does not have such riches, which normally come more abundantly to sinners. Therefore he now says, those whom you can't help with money, help with advice and comfort them with solace. For one is more able to excel in these ways than any of the greatest of potentates. And you would be wise to do this, for the scale of justice is great, and must decide for whom, how much, how long, and of what sort, help is given, either with monetary support or with advice.

30 Ier. 51, 9.

7:22/23 *And do not heed all words that are spoken, lest you hear your servant curse you. For often your own heart knows that you likewise have cursed others.* Make sure to do only those things which have been taught, and strengthened by the help of wisdom, prepare yourself for either good or bad outcomes, and don't worry about what your enemies might say about you, or what kind of reputation you have. For just as a cautious man should not hear his servant complain about him, so he should not want to hear what is said about him in his absence, (for if he did this he would always be troubled and incensed to anger by the muttering of the servant). Therefore it is befitting for a wise man to walk with wisdom following him, and not to dwell upon unfounded rumours. But he teaches by another example that the righteous man ought not to worry what men say, saying, 'just as your conscience knows what you have said about others, and that you have often maligned others, so you ought to pardon others when they think badly of you.' At the same time he teaches that it is difficult to judge for one who has a rod in his eye, not to speak about the rod of another.

31 Cfr. III Reg. 3. 4

7:24/25. *I have proved all this by wisdom: I said, I will be wise; but it was far from me. That which is far off, and exceeding deep, who can find it out?* Just as is attested in the Book of Kings[31] he says that he sought wisdom more than other men, and tried to reach the pinnacle, but the more he sought, the less he found, and in the midst of his confusion, he was surrounded by the darkness if ignorance. But at another time, regarding him who was learned in the Scriptures- the more he wanted to know, the more a greater obscurity arose each day for him. Another meaning of this is: he seems to mean that contemplation of wisdom in this life is like looking in a mirror or at a picture; therefore if I look at my face in the mirror in the future I'll think back to the way it used to be, and then in the liquid pool I'll recognise that I differ greatly from the way I used to be.

7:26/27. *I applied my heart to know, and to search, and to seek out wisdom, and the reason of things, and to know the wickedness of folly, even of foolishness and madness. And I find that woman is more bitter than death, whose heart is snares and nets, and her hands are as bands: whoever pleases God shall escape her; but the sinner shall be taken by her.* The Septuagint here has: "I even applied my heart that I should know". Symmachus has interpreted this saying, 'I have looked into all things with my reasoning to know, to distinguish and to find out.' Since therefore Ecclesiastes had said above that he had tried to know all wisdom and the more he sought it the more it eluded him, now he says even that he sought out another thing in his wisdom, for wickedness precedes all things in human affairs, and that affair is first and foremost in impiety, stupidity, madness, and insanity. He also says that he found woman to be the cause of all evil, since through her, death came into the world and took the most prized spirits of men. And even for all adulterers, it is like there is a coat of mail on their heart, the heart that makes the souls of adolescents soar upwards. And when this happens to the mind of a wretched lover, it pushes him into first position, and he is not allowed to look back at his feet, but like a snare or noose it ensnares the heart of a youth. 'For he has chains around his wrists', which Aquila interpreted as being, 'for his hands are in chains'. For he can convince, but he doesn't have the strength and can't pull himself to those who are unwilling. Those things destroy him, who was righteous and good before God; but the sinner who has been captured will be led down to his death. Let us not think that Solomon held this opinion about women thoughtlessly, he speaks only those things that he has experienced. For this reason he fears God, since women have captured him. And these interpretations are very literal. But according to the spiritual understanding of this passage, either we should take every sin made in general, and call it 'woman' and 'wickedness', for example, she who sits behind the façade of woman in Zechariah above the talent of lead.[32] Or we can take woman to be the devil metaphorically on account of effeminate men; or indeed idolatry, and so that we might proceed more closely, the church or heretics, which calls the fool to itself by reasoning, so that he receives stolen bread, and stolen water, the false sacrament, and is led to be baptised in polluted water.

32 Cfr. Zech. 5, 7.

7:28/30. *Behold, I have found this, says the preacher, counting one by one, to find out the account. Which still my soul seeks, but I have not found it. I have found one man among a thousand, but one woman among all those I have not found. Only this have I found: that God has made man righteous, but he has sought out many inventions.* He says, "I found this", teaching all things diligently, that by sinning little by little, and adding one crime on top of another, we amass a great number of sins for ourselves. '*esebon*' even, which all translate as *logismon* in Greek, according to the ambiguity of the Hebrew language can be said by us to be 'number', 'sum', 'account', and 'consideration'. But, he says, my spirit sought even this question of whether woman is rightly found to be guilty. And although I found scarcely any men to be good, thus so that only one from a thousand can be found, I couldn't even find one woman to be completely good. For all of them have led me not to virtue but to self-indulgence. And because man's heart is predisposed towards wickedness from boyhood, and almost all of us offend God in some way, in this failing of mankind, women are more prone to this fate. The famous poet says about this: "inconstant and always changeable is woman"[33]. And the apostle says, "always learning yet never arriving at the knowledge of the truth"[34]. But he does not condemn this nature as being common to all mankind, or say that God the creator does evil things, because he is the creator of these things, but he warns subtly those who are not able to avoid evil, and says that we are created good by God; but he also says that because we are left with our own free-will to deteriorate into a worse and worse state through our own vices, while we seek greater things

33 Virg. Aen. 4. 569/70.

34 II Tim. 3.7.

and contemplate many things beyond our strength. Differently: while I consider the reason behind each and every one of these verses, I have found no thought, which is not perturbed from outside by wicked thoughts. But in a thousand men I have found one man, who is made in the image of his creator; and not in a thousand of any kind, but of one thousand *men*. There is not a like number of women corresponding to men. In the thousand, those who have not been close to a woman have therefore remained the most pure. But all this must be taken as a metaphor. In many though, who enthuse and every day sweat in their thinking, scarcely can there be found one pure thought, that is worthy of the name of man. We can take thoughts for men though, and women for work, and say that the thoughts of man can only be seen as pure with great difficulty. But since the body does work, it is always mixed up with some fault. But instead of that which we said above interpreting the Hebrew phrase, "one upon another, so that a great accumulation is made" we could either say 'account', or 'thought'; Symmachus interprets this more clearly, saying, "one upon another makes an amount". And we are accustomed to call this complete and neutral, which I sought and had wanted to find. The Hebrews name this in the case of females, just as in the phrase "I sought one from God, this I ask"[35], in place of that which is one.[36]

35 Ps. 26, 4.

36 [lit. "pro eo quod est unum"]

Chapter 8

8:1. Who *is like the wise man? And who knows what things mean? A man's wisdom lights up his face, and the boldness of his face is transformed.* He had taught above that it is hard to find a good man, and he had answered the question to the contrary, saying that men are made good by God, but that they fall into sin because of their own free will. Now he lists what qualities God has given to a good man, to show his glory: wisdom obviously, and reason and providence, and he knows that the secrets that are hidden by God enter his heart. But he is also talking about himself here indirectly, because no one was as wise as Solomon was, and none answered the problems he set. And because his wisdom was praised by all, wisdom which he not only carried on the inside, but also wore on the surface of his skin, and which shone from his face, he moreover imbued all men with the wisdom which shone forth from his visage. Where we have, 'who is like the wise man?' the Septuagint reads: "who knows wise men?" and where we read, 'the boldness of his face is transformed', the Septuagint has, "and the unwise is disliked by his face". And although in fact there are many, who engage themselves in the pursuit of wisdom, it is found with great difficulty, but he is able to tell a wise man though from those, who only seem to be wise. Though too there are even many more, who say that they are able to let themselves tell the secrets of the Scriptures, it is not common however, that one will actually find the true answer. But what follows- "the wisdom of a man will light up his face and the wicked is hated by his face" - can be explained in the way that Paul explains it: "but we all see the glory of God with our face uncovered"[1]. The writer of the Psalms also says, "the light of your face shines down upon us, O Lord"[2]. But he says that the wisdom of man is not different from the wisdom of God. Although it is the wisdom of God, it then begins to be also a part of the human faculty, but only when it is in him who merits wisdom. Every heretic, who defends his false doctrines, shows his foolishness on his face. Then Marcion and Valentinus say that they are of a better nature than the Creator himself! This can be seen in another way, if they contend to hope for this wisdom, but do not already possess it.

8:2/4 *I counsel you: Obey the king's command, and that in the manner of an oath of God. Do not hasten to leave his presence, do not persist in an evil thing; for he can do whatever he pleases. Since a king's word is law, who dare say to him, 'what are*

1 II Cor. 3, 18.

2 Ps. 4,7.

62

3 Ps. 20, 1.

4 Tob. 12,7.

5 Tob. 12,7

you doing?' Here he seems to teach the same as the apostle - that we should obey kings and rulers, which is set out in the Septuagint as a command: "guard the command of the king"; but personally I think he is now talking about that king about whom David says, "Lord, the king will be happy in your virtue"[3]. And in another passage, where it means the one reign of the Father and of the Son, the text reads, "God, give your judgement to the king, and your righteousness to the son of the king".[4] For the Father does not judge each one, but gives each judgement to the Son. Moreover, that king who is the Son of God, is the son of the Father who is the King. Therefore His precepts should be kept, His will done. And this is exactly what is written in the book of Tobit: "it is good to hide the secret of the king"[5]. He warns in particular why we should not ask why God has taught every single thing, but see that teaching as a commandment, and this is what an impious man hastens to fulfil. Then let his will be the same as that of God's law. But because the Septuagint translates this differently, saying, "do not hasten to run away from God's presence", nor his judgement or his word, you must know that God's judgement is written in the divine will. Therefore we ought not to recount to anyone or make public this judgement, which is taken to be sacred and secret from the word of God, nor should we form rash opinions from it. We should not, too, hasten like Moses, to see the face of God, but rather wait a while until He Himself passes by and then we will only see Him passing. Nor too should we do what follows: do not persist in an evil thing, and so on, especially as we understand, like one who has already come into the madness of heresy, or as he, who although having faith in the Church, is still overcome by sins, so that he is unfaithful. Do not persevere in what is wrong, or in swearing, indulgence, greed, or lust. For if you do the king of vices and devil of sins will fashion in you your end, and he will be able to do whatever he wants with you.

6 II Cor. 5, 21

8:5. ***He who obeys the commandment will know no evil; and a wise man will know time and justice.*** Notice here in particular that 'he will know no evil' has been written instead of 'he will not suffer' or even 'evil will not be in him'. Likewise it has also been written about the Saviour, "for he has made him to be sin for us, who knew no sin."[6] Instead of 'evil' too Symmachus interprets this phrase as saying, "he who keeps the commandment will experience no wickedness". But he teaches that we should keep the command of a king, and know why and when he orders.

8:6/7. *For everything has its time and justice, for man's evil overwhelms him. Indeed he does not know what will happen, for when it happens , who will tell him?* Many good and bad things can befall a man, but even a righteous man is not able to know what will befall him, or know the causes and reasons for each thing, (for no one can know what will happen), but he does know that all things are done by God to the advantage of man, and nothing is done without His will. For this is a great sufferance for mankind, since as the poet says: "the mind of man knows not his lot and coming fate"[7]. If he hopes for one thing, then another happens; he expects the enemy to come from one direction and is wounded by a spear from the opposite direction. But here Theodotion and the Septuagint have said, "since the knowledge of man overwhelms him", the Hebrew has 'wickedness' not 'knowledge'. But because the Hebrew letters 'Resh' and 'Daleth' are similar without the serif, instead of *raath* they have read *daat,* that is instead of 'wickedness', 'knowledge'. This is easier to understand if you have knowledge of the language. Note too, that which is written at the end of the verse: 'since he doesn't know what has been, and what will be after him, who will tell him?' I have translated word for word here from the Hebrew text, so that we can see that there is a different meaning, since we are clearly not able to know those things which have already passed away, or those that will be, as they have yet to be done.

7 Virg. Aen. 10, 501.

8:8. *Man is powerless over the spirit-to restrain the spirit; nor is there authority over the day of death; nor discharge in war; and wickedness cannot save the wrong-doer.* Our mind does not have the power to prevent the spirit from being taken from us, and when the spirit leaves to the realm of God, it helps nothing to shut out mouth and hold in our fleeting life. And when we are dead, the enemy of our life will come and we are not able to take any rest. Note too the kings in one age, which destroying all our things irreligiously led us by the hands to our death, but we were taken into the ashes and the earth. Therefore we must not mourn if we cannot know the future and we are often oppressed by more powerful and wicked men, for all things end in death: for the proud and the powerful the same end; he who has devastated all things does not deserve to keep his life when it is taken away. Another meaning could be that the spirit that is the source of life cannot be prevented from leaving any man, this is the rule of mortality. Above too he also spoke of this: "turning, turning goes the wind"[8]. We have no power in the day of our death, but when we are alive our enemy is easily avoided. Similarly he who is in time of war and does not have

8 Eccl. 1,6.

9 Cant. 4, 13

the peace of God, which overpowers all feeling, he will not have any discharge therefrom, about which it is said to a bride, "your discharge is paradise with the fruit of apples"[9]. And because piety will not save him who has it, piety will save the opposite, and impiety can be called the Devil and piety our Lord Jesus Christ.

8:9/11. *All this have I seen; and I applied my mind to see every deed that is done under the sun: there is a time when one man rules over another to his detriment. And then I saw the wicked buried and newly come while those who had done right were gone from the Holy place and were forgotten in the city. This too is vanity! Because the sentence for wrong-doing is not executed quickly- that is why men are encouraged to do evil.* I have dedicated my heart, he says, that I should see all that is done under the sun, and this too, that man takes up arms against man, so that he afflicts and condemns those whom he wants. And so when I began to look upon those things I saw that the impious were dead by such belief and buried, and were deemed holy in the earth, but those who were living were thought to be worthy of the Church, and the temple of God, the bombastic walking above were praised for their wickedness. "For the sinner is praised for the laxity of his soul, and he who is wicked is blessed"[10]. But this happens moreover

10 Ps. 9,24.

because no one dares to confront sinners and God does not immediately give punishment for crimes, but rather postpones, so that we must await our repentance. But since those who sin are not immediately arrested and accused, they think with little regard that their judgement will be in the future, and continue in their crime. We can see how this evidence pertains to certain bishops, who come to power in the Church, and speak ill of those, which had taught and had urged them to follow better pursuits. These men are very often praised after death in the Church, and blessed for those things, which they in all likelihood did not even do, or openly are warned by their successors or the congregation. And even this is vanity, since while they live they do not heed advice and are not immediately visited for their sins, (since none dares accuse his superior), besides they act as if holy and blessed, and as if they are walking in the precepts of the Lord, and they increase their sins one on top of another. Such an accusation of a bishop is difficult. For you see, if he has sinned, it is not believed, and if he is accused, he is not punished.

8:12. *Because a sinner does what is wrong an hundred times and He is patient with him, yet nevertheless I am aware that it will be* *well with those who fear God that they may fear Him.* Because a sinner has done many wicked deeds, this is what is meant by, 'an hundred times': God gives a time for repentance, and does not punish him immediately for his crime, but he waits so that he is converted by his wickedness. I understand how good-willing and forgiving God will be to those who fear Him and tremble at His word. Symmachus translated this passage as, "For a sinner dies wicked, long-life is granted him". More precisely I know that it will be well for those who fear God, who fear His face, but it will not be well for the wicked, and he will not live long, for he does not fear God. And because what Symmachus translated is clear, we can say that the Hebrew word *maath* is what the Septuagint has translated as 'from then on', which we have here as 'an hundred times'. Aquila, Symmachus, and Theodotion have interpreted 'he has died' as "he has sinned and done evil, and is dead", because for that which he sinned, he immediately dies. But according to the interpretation of the Septuagint, instead of 'he is dead' we read 'from then on', and according to that interpretation, the meaning is, 'a sinner does not sin at first when he seems to sin, but already even before he has sinned': "Sinners are estranged from the womb, they have erred since they were in the stomach"[11]. And they ask this that follows-

11 Ps. 57, 4

"they have spoken falsity", just as he explains for a simple understanding, there seems to be no reason that child sinners speak lies as soon as they come out of the womb.

12 Gal. 5,12.

13 II Tim. 4, 14.

8:13. And *it will not be well with the wicked, and he will not live long-like a shadow-because he does not fear God.* He invokes wickedness upon those who do not fear God, and desires that they do not wait long for their punishment, but rather are crucified and immediately put to death, this punishment is for those who merit such a death. This is similar to what the apostle says: "I would that those who annoy us were put to death."[12] And in another place "Alexander the coppersmith did me much evil, may the Lord reward him according to his works."[13] We must ask though how these things are said so mildly. This is very true to the Hebrew meaning of this verse. But we can follow the Septuagint's interpretation, which seems to take another meaning, and says, "and I know, since those who fear God will be well, that they fear his face, and the wicked will not be well, and his day will not be long in shadows, who does not fear God." He could have said this: 'let there also be those things which I considered a little earlier', but I know clearly that those fearing God will be well; "for the face of God is above those who do wickedness"[14]. And the wicked will not be well, for he does not fear God and his days will not be longer in shadows. This is the day of his life, which is like a shadow for the living. Not by this do those who live for a long time lengthen their days, but they make them great with the number of their good deeds. As if confessing himself to be a sinner, Jacob says about this: "few and wicked are these days of mine"[15]. And confessing in the Psalm he says, "my days are inclined like shadows, and I am like the hay of the field"[16]. Not because he has sought a long life in the present world, in which all that we live is brief and looks lie shadow: "for man walks in His likeness"[17], but because he fears the future, lest the length of his life, if it is indeed life, should be short.

8:14. There *is a futility that takes place on earth: sometimes there are righteous men who are treated as if they had done according to the deeds of the wicked; and there are wicked men who are treated as if they had done the deeds of the righteous. I declared, this, too, is vanity.* Amongst other vanities, which are borne in the world by good and bad events, even this I have found to be vain, since those things often happen to the righteous which ought to happen to the wicked, and the wicked live happily in the world that you would think that they were the more righteous! He gives the example in the Gospel of the rich courtier and poor Lazarus.[18] The seventy-second Psalm also talks about the matter of why bad things happen to good men and vice-versa. But where we read, 'there is a futility that takes place on earth', Symmachus translates this fully, saying, "it is difficult to understand what is done on earth". The Hebrews interpret the righteous who suffer wickedness as the sons of Aaron, and Manasseh, because the former died while sacrificing, and the latter was restored to power after much wickedness and captivity.

8:15. So *I praised enjoyment, for man has no other aim under the sun but to eat, drink, and be joyful; and this will accompany him in his toil during the days of his life which God has given him beneath the sun.* I have interpreted this more fully above, and now I shall just speak cursorily. He is allowed to prefer to eat and drink, which is the enjoyment (and must be short and end quickly) in the dire-straits of his life, and in light of those things, which are seen to happen unfairly in the world, (since man seems to have only this in

14 Ps. 33, 17.

15 Gen. 47, 9.

16 Ps. 101, 12.

17 Ps. 38, 7

18 Cfr. Luc. 16, 19-31

67

return for his toil), he enjoys only modest recompense. But if the interpretation is read in the way it has been written, it reproves the wretched, the fasting and the hungry, the thirsty and the mourners, whom the Lord calls blessed in the Gospel[19]. And we regard food and drink spiritually and above this happiness, which we are scarcely able to find in the toil of our life. But because these things are expressed in this way, as I have said, the following verse shows this too, which says, "I dedicated my heart to seeing wisdom and work", since clearly men work on earth, and consider deeply the Scriptures day and night in this way so that sleep flees from their eyes, in return for their study.

8:16/17. *When I applied my heart to see wisdom and work which takes place on earth- for even day or night its eyes see no sleep. And I perceived all the work of God. Indeed man cannot fathom the events that occur under the sun, inasmuch as man tries strenuously to search, but cannot fathom it. And even though a wise man should presume to know, he cannot know it.* He searches for the causes and understanding of the world, why this or that is done, and for what reason the world is steered by good or bad turns of events; why one is born blind and frail, another born healthy and with sight; why one is poor, another rich; why one is of high birth, another inglorious. Nothing else is of use, unless he is tortured in his search, and has an argument instead of anguish, but he does not find what he is looking for. And when he says that he knows, then he has the beginning of ignorance in him, and starts to sink into deeper madness. But he shows later that justice is the cause of all things, why things happen the way they do, but that those causes hide in secret and are not able to be understood by men.

Chapter 9

9:1. For *all this I noted and I sought to ascertain all this: that the righteous and the wise together with their actions are in the Hand of God; whether love or hate man does not know; all preceded them.* Symmachus also interprets this more clearly, saying: I kept all these things in my heart so that I could expound all things, since the righteous and the wise, along with their works are in the hand of God. And besides neither friendship, nor hatred is known to man; yet all things are not certain in their presence, because they happen similar to all, both to the righteous and to the wicked alike. More precisely the meaning is this: I dedicated my heart even to this and wanted to know whom it is that God loves, and whom He hates. And I found too that even the work of the righteous is in the hand of God, but though, whether they are loved by God or not, now they know it cannot be and they remain undecided as to whether they should keep on doing what they are doing until it is approved, or pray. In the future therefore they will know and all will be on their faces, that is 'will precede them' when they leave this life. Knowledge of that matter then will come to them, since then is the judgement, but now the struggle. And whosoever remains confused as to whether they should keep on through the love of God, as Job, or through hate, as several sinners, will not be able to know for certain.

9:2. All *things come alike to all; the same fate awaits the righteous and the wicked, the good and the clean and the unclean, the one who brings a sacrifice and the one who does not. As is the good man so is the sinner, as is the one who swears, so is the one who fears an oath.* These things which in themselves are neither good nor bad but are called 'in-between' by the wise, (since equally things happen to both the righteous and the wicked), they perturb each single man, especially as to why they should happen thus, and therefore do not think they are being judged, while there will be a distinction between all things in the future when they have been done, yet now all things are confused. But he says: "there is one outcome for the just and the unjust", he means either the outcome of hardships or of death, and therefore they do not know the kingdom of God nor His hate. Those who bring sacrifice and those who do not, and others in contrast who are not listed here must be seen in a spiritual understanding, according to that verse which says, "sacrifice to God with a troubled spirit"[1].

9:3/4. *This is an evil about all things that are done under the sun: that the same fate awaits all Therefore the heart of man is full of evil; and madness is in their heart while they live; and after that, they go to the dead.* Symmachus interprets this in his usual clearer way, saying, "but even the heart of mankind is filled with wickedness and impudence like their heart in life". But all of them succumb to death, for who is able to continually live forever? The Scripture has the same meaning regarding this. I said a little earlier, that when both good and bad things happen equally to everyone, there is no difference between good and bad, for we are taken from this life by indiscriminate death. Nonetheless we are filled with wrongdoings and impudence and wickedness, and after all these trials in life we are suddenly taken by death and afterwards we cannot consort with the living. Or indeed it could mean this: since the same difficulties afflict both the just and the unjust, men are therefore provoked to commit sins. Then after he has tried all things, which are done in vain, while he is unknowing, he descends to the world of the dead. *For he who is attached to all living has hope, a live dog is better than a dead lion.*

9:5/6. *For the living know that they will die, but the dead know nothing at all; there is no more reward for them, their memory is forgotten. Their love, their hate, their jealousy have already perished- nor will they ever again have a share in whatever is done beneath the sun.* Since he has said above that the heart of man is filled with wickedness and impudence, and after all things, his life comes to an end in death, then now he completes this by saying that he has discovered that while men live, they are able to become righteous, but after death are given no opportunity to do good work. For the sinner who lives can be better than the dead and righteous man, if he wishes to convert to his virtues. Or indeed as for him, who threw himself into wickedness, power, and impudence, then died: any poorest beggar is better than him. Why? Because the living can carry out good work in the fear of death, but the dead can do nothing to add to that which they took away from their life when they died. And all things are forgotten, just as it is written in the Psalm: "I have been given to forget, though dead from my heart"[2]. But even their enjoyment, hatred and jealousy, and all that they were able to hold in their time, comes to an end with their death; nor can they do anything now in their righteousness or sin, or add to their virtues, or to their vices. Certain men though can argue against this explanation, asserting that we can even grow after death, and equally decrease, and quoting that verse which says, "and they will not share yet in all that is done under the sun", and they

1 Ps. 50, 19.

2 Ps. 30,13.

70

understand it in this way, so that they say that they have no communion in this world, and under this sun that we can see. But they say that they do have it in another world, about which the Saviour says, "I am not of this world"[3], and under the sun of justice, but I have not excluded this theory, which contends that after we leave this earth, we are able to offend reasoning creatures, and deserve what we get. My Hebrew tutor thought differently of the verse, which says, "a living dog is better than a dead lion". He explained it in this way according to the beliefs of his people: an unlearned man is more useful, he who still lives and can teach, than a trained teacher who is now dead. Because of the text he understands it to mean any one dog is better than many teachers, and the lion is Moses, or any other prophet. But because I don't like this explanation I prefer a better one; and Chananaea to whom it is said: "your faith saves you"[4], we say he is a dog according to the Gospel. But a dead lion, for the people of circumcision is just the same as for Balaam, the prophet, who says, "behold the people shall rise up as a great lion, and shall lift up himself as a young lion"[5]. Therefore we are a living dog amongst the other nations; but the Jewish people which has been left by God, is a dead lion. And that living dog is seen as better in God's eyes than a dead lion. For we who are living know the Father, the Son, and the Holy Spirit. The dead though can know nothing, or await any recompense and profit, since their memory is complete. They don't remember what they ought to know, and God does not remember them. Enjoyment too, for which they often loved God, will die, and hatred as well, about which they say boldly, "surely I hate those who hate You, O Lord, and am I not grieved with those that rise up against You?"[6]. And there does not exist their jealousy, similar to the Phinees, and the knees of Matathia trembled.[7] But it is very clear that a part of them is not in that world, for they are not able to say, "my part is the Lord".[8]

9:7/8. *Go, eat your bread with joy and drink your wine with a glad heart, for God has already approved your deeds. Let your garments always be white, and your head never lack oil.* Regarding the passage until that verse where he says: 'like fish caught in a fatal net, like birds seized in a snare, so are men caught in the moment of disaster when it falls upon them suddenly'.[9] Before I discuss them individually, it will be useful to link them together, so that it can be seen how all pertain to the same meaning. Because in a preceding chapter he had said that after men

3 Ioh. 8, 23.

4 Matth. 9, 23.

5 Num. 23,24.

6 Ps. 138, 21.

7 Cfr. I Mach. 2, 24-6.54.

8 Ps. 72, 26.

9 Eccl. 9, 12.

71

10 Verg. Aen. XI. 104

have died they are cut off from the heart of the living, and no one loves or hates them, as according to the poet, who says, "there is no struggle from the dead, who lack breath"[10]. And because they can do no more under the sun, now he introduces the idea of human madness and habit, whereby men of this world encourage themselves in turn to enjoy good things; and *prosopopoiian*, using this in the manner of rhetoricians and poets, saying: "O man, since there is nothing for you after death, and death herself hears not my complaint, and while you live this brief life, take pleasure in enjoyment, hold feasts, suppress your worries with wine, and understand, since they are all given by God to be used by you. Wear white clothes, and let your head smell of ointments, and whichever woman pleases you, enjoy her embrace, thus lead this empty and vain life in empty and vain pleasure. For you will not have anything more than this, which you enjoy. Whatever you like, grasp quickly, lest it disappears. You shouldn't fear the vain things mentioned, for the reason for each individual work, either good or bad, will be given to you in the world of the dead. And there is no wisdom in death, no

11 i.e.Eratosthenes

sense of this life after passing away. He also says that Epicurus, Aristippus, and the philosophers of Cyrene[11], and other of the philosophical flock hold this belief. But I prefer my own ideas, and I do not find, as some people think incorrectly, that everything happens by chance, and good and bad fate plays on human lives. I rather believe that everything happens by the order of God. For the fast runner should not think of his running when he runs, nor a strong man have faith in his strength, or a wise man think amassing great riches and wealth is prudent; the learned and well-spoken should not be able to find himself amongst a flattering crowd because of his eloquence and learning, but by attributing all things to be done by God. And unless he has ruled all things in his own judgement, and built his own home, then they worked in vain, who built it. Except if he built a city, those, who watch over it, will stay awake in vain. For it is not as they think it is, that there is one outcome and uncertainty in this life, since they do not think so, who are suddenly taken away by death and taken to their judgement. And just as fish are caught by a spear or in nets, and birds are ensnared in a noose whilst they fly through the air unknowing, in the same way men are led away to eternal prayer on account of their merits, when sudden death comes and judges against them, who thought all things in life happened by uncertainty. This is similar to that meaning by which we wanted to understand all things in brief. Now he speaks not as if from another person's mouth, but for himself, each phrase must be looked at on its own: "Go, eat your bread with joy and drink your wine with a glad heart, for God has already approved your deeds". Since you learned that all things end with death, and that repentance is not in the world of the dead, and that there is no recourse to virtues, while you are in that situation, then hasten, struggle, repent, while you still have the time. For God acknowledges repentance freely. Another meaning could be, that simply understanding is of use, according to that verse, which says, "whether therefore you eat, or drink, or whatever you do, do all to the glory of God."[12] And in another place: drink wine with warning"[13]. For he who uses up more than his means does not have true happiness and a good heart. But it is better to think this: the works of this man pleased God, nonetheless he had need of bread and wine, because he has been spurned from the vineyard of Sorek. Therefore this teaching has been given to us, as he says, "if you desire wisdom, then keep the commandments and the Lord shall give it to you"[14]. Let us then keep the commandments and we will be able to find bread and wine for the spirit. But he who does not keep the commandments prides himself in the abundance of his bread and wine, and Isaiah says to him, "do not even say, I know it, you do not know, or recognise, and your ears have not heard from the beginning, for I knew that you would deal very treacherously"[15]. More precisely as it is said in the interpretation given in the Septuagint: Come, eat your bread in happiness, this is the word of Ecclesiastes, who even speaks in the Gospel: "If any man thirst, let him come unto me, and drink."[16] And in Proverbs: "Come, eat of my bread, and drink of the wine. Let your clothes be white forever and may your hair be oiled[17]. He therefore says, have a clean body and be merciful. Or in this way: 'let there not be a time in which you do not have white clothes, beware lest you by accident put on clothes that are not clean'. A known sinner was once described to have enjoyed dirty clothes. But you should put on the light, not the malediction, which was also written about Judah: "let a

12 I Cor. 10, 31.

13 'Quotation of uncertain origin.'

14 Eccli. 1, 33.

15 Is. 48, 7.8.

16 Ioh. 7, 37.

17 Prov. 9, 5.

curse be worn like clothes"[18]. Wear by your skin mercy, kindness, humility, mildness and patience. And when you have been stripped, as an old man, of your work, take on new work, which is renewed each day. He also says, "and let your hair not lack oil", you must remember that this is the nature of ointment, that it reflects light and reduces the work of tiredness. It is spiritual ointment, the ointment of exultation, about which is written: "therefore God, your God, has anointed you with the oil of gladness above your friends"[19]. This oil must gladden our face. This oil must be put on the head of a faster, for sinners cannot have it, about whom it is said, "they have not been closed, neither bound up, neither mollified with ointment"[20]. But they have a different ointment, which the righteous man abhors, saying, "the oil of a sinner will not stain my head"[21]. Heretics have this oil and wish to pour it over the heads of their beguilers.

18 Ps. 109, 18.

19 Ps. 45, 7.

20 Is. 1, 6.

21 Ps. 140, 5

22 Prov. 4, 8.

9:9. *Enjoy life with the wife you love through all the fleeting days of your life that He has granted you under the sun, all of your futile existence; for that is your compensation in life and in your toil which you exert under the sun.* Follow wisdom and knowledge of the Scriptures, while you are joined in matrimony to your wife, as it is said in Proverbs: "love her and she will serve you: embrace her and she will embrace you too"[22]. But the day of vanity, the day of this world means nothing. The apostle mentions this too, and he says, "live life with the woman that you love", but this is said in ambiguity, either live or contemplate life both you yourself and your wife with you, for you will not be able to live life alone without such a wife, or consider each one and live life, and consider the woman in the days of your vanity. And he words this carefully, so that we seek the true life with our wife and wisdom in the days of our vanity. For this is our lot and the fruit of our toil, if we, retired, are able to find this true life.

9:10. Whatever *you are able to do with your strength, do it. For there is neither doing, nor reckoning, nor knowledge, nor wisdom in the grave where you are going.* Do whatever you are presently able to do, and toil at it, because when you go down to the world of the dead there will be no place for repentance. Similar to this is what is taught by the Saviour: "work hard, while there is still day left; for night will come, when none is able to work"[23], but he says this: "to the grave where you are going", remember too that you believe Samuel was also in the grave, and before the advent of Christ, all men were retained by the law of the dead, however holy they were. More precisely, the holy were retained after the resurrection of the Lord in vain in the grave, and the apostle notes this, remarking, "it is better to die and be with Christ"[24]. But he is with Christ, so that he might not be held back in the grave.

9:11. Once *more I saw under the sun that the race is not won by the swift; nor the battle by the strong, nor does bread come to the wise, riches to the intelligent, nor favour to the learned; but time and death will happen to them all.* He who is bound by manacles and by heavy lead chains is oppressed: "for wickedness sits upon a talent of lead"[25], and in the Psalm it says, "they weigh on me like a heavy burden"[26]. It is not talking about that race, about which is said, "I took up the race, and I kept my faith"[27]. But that man is swift and his spirit is not weighed down, nonetheless even he is not able to arrive at the goal without God helping him. But when there has been a war against adverse leaders, about whom it is written, "make war sacred"[28], even a strong man will not be able to win with his own strength. This is also true of the sons of man and the wise who cannot have living bread for the spirit, except through encouraging wisdom: "Come, eat my bread"[29]. And since there are riches, about which the apostle says, "riches come through good deeds"[30], and in another place, "you have been made rich in every utterance and knowledge"[31]; it must be understood that a wise man cannot amass these riches, unless he receives them from God, who possesses them. In another place these riches are mentioned too: "redemption of the spirit for man is his own riches"[32]. However learned a man is, he will not be able to find grace too, unless accompanied by wisdom and given by God. Paul also knows this: "I worked more than all men," he says, "yet not I but the grace of God which was with me". Then again he says, "His grace in me was not in vain". And right to the end man does not know when the time will come, when the unknown fate and end of all things will come. This reading is according to *anagoge*. But in order to explain this more easily, I should mention that the epistle to the Romans agrees with this verse: "So then it is not of him that wants, nor of him that runs, but of God that shows mercy."[33] He also says this: "there is no bread for the wise", this example is proved every day for many people, who although they are very wise, still do not have the necessary sustenance for life. And: "there is no grace for the knowledgeable". For you may see in the Church that

23 Ioh. 9, 4.

24 Phil. 1, 23.

25 Zach. 5, 7.

26 Ps. 37, 5.

27 II. Tim. 4, 7

28 Ier. 6, 4.

29 Prov. 9, 5.

30 I Tim. 6, 18.

31 I Cor. 1, 5.

32 Prov. 15, 8.

33 Rom. 9, 16

75

the ignorant and unskilled prosper. And this is both because they have nourished their boldness, and followed the fluency of their tongue, while they do not think about what they say, they think that they are wise and learned, and as if they have the greatest favour of the populous, which delights and is brought together more by more polished words. On the other hand a learned man lies in obscurity and suffers persecution; and not only does he not have grace in the people's eyes, but also fades away through poverty and hunger. But these things happen because all things occur by uncertainty, and there is no retribution of merit in this world, but in the future.

9:12. *For man does not even know his time, like fish caught in a fatal net, like birds seized in a snare, so are men caught in the moment of disaster when it falls upon them suddenly.* I have already said above, that while men are yet unknowing, either disaster or death befalls them. More precisely we should look at this as allegory, that the realm of the sky is similar to a net cast into the sea; and on the other hand heretics have nets, in which they capture fish, leading to their death. Their net though is affable language, flattering speeches, feigned or forced fasting, poor clothes, and an imitation of virtues. And if they begin to argue about the divine and raise their face to the heavens to seek the heights of God, then they cast a noose into the heavenly abodes. So just as fish and birds are seized of a sudden by such a net, and by such a noose, so wickedness is increased many times and the kindness of many fails; and the signs and portents are seen in such a way as to entice even the chosen of God if possible. See too those men of the Church, who are called the children of men, and are of modest faith, and who can be overcome quickly. Note too, that the term *sons of men* is used throughout the whole book, and the Hebrew has *sons of man*, this is 'the sons of Adam'. And almost all scripture is filled with this idiom that sees the sons of Adam as the sons of all men.

9:13/15. *This, too, I have observed about wisdom under the sun, and it affected me profoundly: there was a small town with only a few inhabitants; and a mighty king came upon it and surrounded it, and built great siege works over it. Present in the city was a poor wise man who by his wisdom saved the town. Yet no one remembered that poor man.* While some people say that all things are uncertain, and that the righteous have no more than the wicked, I see even the greatest wisdom in this verse, because it happens repeatedly that there is a small township with only a few inhabitants, and it is surrounded by an army of a very powerful enemy, and the people inside is killed by the siege and by hunger. And suddenly and unexpectedly a poor man is found, who has more wisdom than all the rich men, than all those powerful and pompous men who are in danger, and who fear the siege. And he thinks, seeks and finds an answer as to how the town might be saved from the oppressors. But O ungrateful oblivion of men, after they were freed from bondage and released from captivity, and the freedom was given back to the fatherland, no one remembers that wise old man, no one gives thanks for their salvation, but all show honour to the rich, who were able to do nothing to help when in time of danger. My Hebrew tutor interpreted this passage differently: the small town, he says, is man, who even amongst learned men is called less clean. And the few men in the town, are the members by which the man shields and covers himself. But when a great king comes against it, that is the devil, and he searches for a place by which he might break through, and in the town is found a poor and wise man, that is the calm thought of that man on the inside, and that is what saves the town, which is surrounded and besieged by the enemy. And the man has been saved from danger, or persecution, or disaster, or any other kind of adverse sin. But that man on the outside, who is the enemy of the wise and poor man on the inside, he does not remember the poor man, nor does he remember his promises, but yet enjoys his freedom. Differently: the small town and the few inhabitants in it is the Church in comparison to the whole world. And the great king the devil often comes against it, not because he is great, but because he thought to be great, and he surrounds the Church with a siege or persecution, or with another kind of disaster. He finds in it a poor man who is wise, that is our Lord Jesus Christ, who was made poor for us and is wisdom itself. And that poor man frees the town with his wisdom. How many times do we see a reclining lion in a trap with rich men, this is with the politicians and leaders of our time, who come against the Church, but fail at the wisdom of that poor man? And when this poor man has won and the town is restored to peace, scarcely anyone remembers him, scarcely any of his requests are heard, but giving in to all indulgence and pleasure, the inhabitants seek riches that are not necessary.

9:16. So *I said: wisdom is better than might, although a poor man's wisdom is despised and his words go unheeded.* Although no one remembers a poor wise man, and everyone is happy, and admires power and riches; I however admire this despised wisdom according to all of the interpretations given above, and the words which none thinks worthy to be heard.

9:17. The *gentle words of the wise are heard above the shouts of a king over fools.* Whosoever you see in the Church declaiming and arousing applause by whatever refinery or charm, he who shakes off his laughter and incites the crowd to feigned happiness, know that this is a sign of foolishness, equally of him who speaks, and of those who listen to him. For the words of the wise are heard in peace and respectful silence. He who is foolish and is powerful speaks to fools and cannot hear himself because of either the noise of his own voice or that of the applauding crowd.

9:18. And *wisdom is better than weapons, but a single rogue can ruin a great deal of good.* Now he also takes wisdom in preference to strength and says that it is worth more in battle than weapons. But if there is one fool, however small and worthless, he will repeatedly destroy riches and great wealth by his stupidity. But because the Hebrew can also be read as: 'and he who sins once, will lose much goodness', much righteousness will be lost in return and virtues will follow in turn, and he who has one, has all[34]; and he who sins at one time, leaves himself open to all vices[35].

34 Cfr. Cic de Offic. II, 35.

35 Cfr. Iac. 2, 10.

Chapter 10

10:1. Dead *flies putrefy the perfumer's oil; a little folly outweighs wisdom and honour.* Here he gives an example to illustrate the idea expressed above, in which he says that many good things can be outweighed by one fool, since one evil mixed with good in this way will pollute the greater part of it, just as flies if they die in oil, make it lose its colour and smell. And since wisdom is often mixed with cleverness and prudence has wickedness, he teaches that we must search out wisdom alone, or that it be mixed with the innocence of doves. Let us then be prudent to the good, and simple in the face of the wicked. And this is the meaning: let the righteous man have little simplicity on account of his having too much suffering, and while he keeps his retribution for God, he seems foolish, and does wickedness at once in vindication under the guise of prudence. Another meaning could be those flies that according to Isaiah inhabit a part of the river of Egypt, and destroy the sweetness of oil and according to one source leave the smell of their uncleanness[1]. The chief of these flies is called Beelzebub of the demons, and is interpreted as either 'the idol of flies' or 'the man of the flies', or 'he who has flies'[2].

10:2/3. *A wise man's mind tends to his right; while a fool's mind tends to his left. Even on the road as the fool walks, he lacks sense, and proclaims to all that he is a fool.* And in the Gospel it is taught that a wise man's left does not know what his right is doing. And when we are hit on the right side of the face, we do not show the left cheek to he who hit us, but the other one. For a wise man does not have a left side in him, but is in fact completely the right side. And when the Saviour comes to judge us, the lambs will stand on the right, and the goats on the left. It is written in the prophets that "the Lord knows the ways to the right, which are wrong, and actually lead to the left."[3]. Therefore he who is wise always thinks about the future, because it leads him to the right. But he who is foolish always thinks of the present, because it is set in the left. What follows has also been said by the philosopher poet, who says, "the right leads to the walls of the lower world, this is our path to Elysium, but the left is for the wicked. That gives out punishments and sends people down to the nether regions"[4]. Firmianus of our time in the famous work of his Institute recalls the passage about left and right, and argues that this is about virtues and about vices.[5] And we shouldn't think that this is contrary to that passage, which says, "do not go to the right, nor to

1 Cfr. Is. 7, 18.

2 Cfr. Matth. 12, 24.

3 Prov. 4, 27.

4 Virg. Aen. 6, 541/543.

5 Lactant. Divin. Instit. VI, 3,6- CSEL 19, p.486, 166sqq.

79

6 Prov. 4, 27.

7 Cfr. Eph. 2, 2; 6, 12.

8 Ps. 18, 4

the left"[6]. In the first passage the right is taken to mean good; but in the second it is not just right but also the decline to the right. We should not know more than we need to know, since virtues are in the middle and all excess in a vice. In the following verse though he says, "but on the path that the fool walks, his heart is in need", and he says: "all is foolishness" or "all are fools". This is the meaning: A fool hopes that all others sin as he himself sins, and judges all others by his own standards. Then Symmachus has interpreted it in this way: but when the fool walks along the road, he supposes that all are stupid as he is. But the Septuagint has another meaning, which says, 'all things which he thinks are foolish, are the most vain'.

10:4. If *the anger of a ruler flares up against you, do not leave your place, for defence appeases great offences.* Now the Scripture mentions the chief of that world, the creator of the darkness and he who toils for the sons of despair, whom the apostle also recalls.[7] For if he rises in our heart and the spirit of bad thoughts is wounded, we ought not to give way, but fight against the worst thoughts and free ourselves from the greatest sins, so that we do not fill our work with that thought, since it is one thing in thought, another in the deed of sinning. Reference to this great sin can also be found in the Psalm: "if they had not conquered me, I would be clean and purified from the greatest crime"[8]. Symmachus translates the Hebrew word *marphe* as all the others do: *iama*, that is, 'cleanliness' or 'neatness'. He has interpreted the meaning too, and he says, "if the spirit of a ruler defeats you, do not move from your place; since virtue wins over the greatest sin". That is, if the devil entices your mind and incites you to lust, do not follow the thought of sin and flattering desire, but stand firm and fast and extinguish the flame of desire with the cold of chastity. My Hebrew tutor suspected certain things about this passage for a reason I do not know. If you take any high-up position in the world, or are appointed a post higher than the other people, do not let go of your former works and start to forget your former virtues, or cease from your previous work, because the cure for sins is born out of doing good things, and not from pompous and overflowing rank.

10;5/7. *There is an evil that I have observed in the world as if it were an error proceeding from the ruler: folly is placed on lofty heights, while rich men sit in low places. I have seen slaves on horses and nobles walking on foot like slaves.* Where we read "as if it were an error proceeding from the ruler" Aquila, Theodotion

9 Cfr. Horat.
Epod. IV, 14.

10 Hab. 3, 8.

11 Eccli. 27, 29.

12 Ps. 7, 16.

and the Septuagint have interpreted this as "as if not of their own will", that is *hos akousian*, from the face of the ruler. Symmachus agrees with this, saying, "the fool is placed in great elevation, but humble riches remain fixed." And he remembers that he has seen this wickedness in this time, because the judgement of God seems to be unjust. And it happens either through not knowing, or without his will, that either in therulers of the world, or in the leadership of the Church, often these men, who are rich in words and wisdom, rich too in good deeds, remain ignoble and foolish holding a position in the Church. But this happens in front of his face, he who has power in that time, while he oppresses the powerful and learned men, and he does not let them come out in public, but those whom he knows to be foolish in the Church he makes greater, so that the blind are led by the blind into pitfalls. The following verse also has this meaning: "I have seen slaves on horses and nobles walking on foot like slaves". Because these men are slaves of vices and sins, or are so humble, that they are thought to be slaves by other men, they are suddenly inflated by the devil's pompousness, and they wear out the public roads with their ponies[9]. And each noble or wise man that is oppressed by poverty takes the road and occupation of slaves. The Hebrew seems to say that ignorance seems to leave the face of the powerful and rulers. He explains this as God, because men think that in this inequality of matter He is not acting justly, and judging as is correct. More precisely, some men believe as their predecessors do that there must be judgement so that He himself is powerful, a topic that is mentioned before these verses: if a ruler comes up against you, do not give way. Should we not be sad therefore if we seem to be humble in this world, and know from the face of the devil, that the foolish are raised and the rich thrown down? If we know that slaves have the ranks of their masters and rulers do the work of their slaves. Remember though that this horse is seen in a good context, just as in the verse, which says, "and riding will be your salvation".[10]

10:8. He *who digs a pit will fall into it, and he who breaks down a wall will be bitten by a snake.* This is partly unambiguous and partly to be understood in a more complicated way. Since elsewhere Solomon also says, "he that sets a trap will be caught in it"[11]. And in the seventh Psalm: "he laid out a pond and dug it out, and then he fell into the hole he had made"[12]. But the wall and the fence as well are the doctrines of the Church, and the institution set up by the apostles and prophets. And whoever knocks them down or wants them to come to an end is bitten by a snake where he is not looking. Amos writes about this snake: "if he goes down into the underworld, I will order a snake to kill him"[13].

13 Am. 9, 3.

10:9. He *who moves about stones will be hurt by them; he who splits logs will be endangered by them.* In Zechariah sacred stones are moved about the earth.[14] For they do not stay firm in their place, but revolve, and always inclining to other places, they hasten to move away. The Saviour also teaches about these living stones in the city of the Apocalypse[15], and the apostle doesn't forget to mention the building of the Church. Therefore if anyone doing wrong by their heresy, should take away those stones from the building of the Church, then he will suffer torture afterwards. Aquila and Symmachus write about this man, and where we have 'he who moves about stones, will suffer from them', both write, "he who moves stones, will be wounded by them". But because the Scripture says very clearly, "he who moves about stones", or 'moves stones', he does not add 'good' or 'bad'. Moreover and to the contrary it must be understood, that the man of the Church seemingly a bishop and elder, (if we are taking this according to the mandate of Leviticus), took a stone away from the house of lepers, and was obliterated in dust and ashes.[16] And he will suffer for this himself, because he was forced to take away a stone from the Church of Christ and saying, (according to the apostle), "to weep with the weeping, to mourn with the mourners"[17], and "who is weak, and I burn not?"[18]. Also cutting wood, he will be endangered by it. Heretics are non-fruit-bearing wood, and copse that do not bear fruit. Pertaining to this too is that we must not plant a glade in the house of God, and leafy openings, that is arbours of such sounding words are scorned. However learned and wise a man may be therefore who chops this wood with the sword of speech, he will be endangered by it, unless he diligently pays attention. This is similar to what follows, this will happen, "if iron is shaped" and its appearance is changed. This means that if his argument is found to be weaker, or if he does not have a point, in which each argument is well balanced, then the argument of his heart is blunt. Then the strength of wickedness will come upon him and fortify him. For this is what the Septuagint interprets this passage to mean: it says, "and he is fortified by strength, and he will begin to have more wisdom than strength; his wisdom will become strong, and superfluous, but it will not help him who possesses it.

14 Cfr. Zach. 9, 16.

15 Cfr. Apoc. 21, 18-27

16 Cfr. Lev. 14, 45.

17 Rom. 12, 15.

18 II Cor. 11, 29

10:10. If *a blade is blunt and one has not sharpened the edge, nevertheless it strengthens the warriors. Wisdom is a more powerful skill.* If someone, he says, has seen himself lose knowledge of the Scriptures through negligence, and the shrewdness of his intelligence has been blunted, nonetheless he remains disturbed, and he would be just as he had been when he started. But it happens, meanwhile, that he that has a little knowledge is led into pride and stops learning and reading, and little by little takes away from that which now adds nothing to him. Thus the heart of the pupil remains empty, and a blade that has been sharpened is made blunt. For rest and laziness are like a kind of rust of wisdom. So then if anyone has suffered this, let him not despair the remedy for his health, but let him go to his teacher and be instructed again by him, and then after much toil and hard work, and a great deal of much sweat, he will be able to regain that wisdom that he had lost. And this is what is said in the Hebrew more to the point: he will be strengthened by might, that is, by toil, by sweat, by hard work, and daily reading, then wisdom will follow suit, and his toil will come to an end, so that he might be able to receive wisdom once more.

10:11. *If the snake bites because it has not been charmed, then there is no advantage to the charmer's art.* The meaning of this is very apparent: the serpent and the disparager are of the same ilk. For just as the hidden snake bites and injects its poison, so too the other disparages in private, and he pours out the poison of his heart against his brother, and there will be nothing between him and the serpent. For although the tongue of man was created for benediction and encouragement of others, the disparager makes it equal to that of the serpent, while he uses his virtues to bad purposes. Another meaning of this is, that if the serpent devil should bite anyone secretly, and he doesn't know it, he infects him with the poison of sin; and if he who has been struck keeps silent, and does not repent, and does not want to confess his wound to his teacher and brother, they who want to encourage him and see to it that he gets better, are not able to be of any use to him. For if an ill man is ashamed to confess his wound to a doctor, the doctor will not be able to cure what he does not know exists.

10:12. *The words of a wise man win favour, but a fool's lips devour him.* Foolishness, if it is happy in its rusticity, will know less evil. But now he wages war against wisdom, and whatever prudence he sees in a learned man, he does not take to be incited by enthusiasm. For a wise man speaks words of knowledge, words of thanks, which are of use to those that hear them, but the lips of a fool do not receive what is said, as it is said; on the contrary they try to trip up a wise man and make him similar to a fool. And in fact a wise man is taught when a foolish man speaks in his ear, and you could almost say that his words are lost in the deep swell. Therefore he is blessed, who speaks in the ear of a wise man.

10:13/14. *His talk begins as foolishness and ends as evil madness. The fool prates on and on, but man does not know what will be; and who can tell him what will be after him?* So far the discussion has been about the fool, whose lips teach the wise man, or according to another interpretation, his lips make himself corrupt. The beginning and the end of his speech are foolishness and evil madness; or as Symmachus has translated it, confusion, or some kind of inconsistency of words. For while he doesn't keep to the one opinion, he thinks he can escape sin in the many arguments he speaks at the same time. But he does not remember all those who have gone before him, and does not know what will happen after him, and so is confused in ignorance and the darkness, promising himself false knowledge; by this he thinks that he is wise, and that he is learned, if he uses lots of words. This can be taken to refer to the heretics, who do not heed the words of wise men, but continue to argue different sides so they intertwine the beginning and end of their speech in vanity, confusion, and madness; and though they know nothing, they speak more than they know.

10:15. *The toil of fools exhausts them, as one who does not know the way to town.* Join these lines with the verse above; either to those verses that speak in general about fools, who know not God, or in particular to that one which argues about heretics. Read in Plato for example: unravel the tricks of Aristotle, read Zeno and Carneas more diligently, and you will prove to be true what is written here: the toil of fools exhausts them. For they seek the truth in fact with all their enthusiasm, but since they have no leader or anyone to lead the way on their journey, they are led by their human instincts to think that they can understand wisdom, and thus they do not arrive at the town; the Psalm speaks of this too: "Lord, you will scatter their image in your town"[19]. For the Lord will scatter in the town all shadows and strange appearances or characters, in which they clothe themselves in their many doctrines. In another place the Psalm says of this: "the force of a river causes the city of God to rejoice"[20]. And in the Gospel: "a town built on a mountain

19 Ps. 72, 20.

20 Ps. 45, 5.

21 Matth. 5, 14.

22 Is. 27, 3.
(According to
the LXX.)

23 Ps. 107, 4.

cannot be hidden"[21]. And in Isaiah: "I am a strong city, a city which is attacked"[22]. And all the wise men and heretics of this world are trying to attack this city of truth and wisdom, although it is strong and fortified. And that which I have said about philosophers can also be said of heretics, that they toil in vain, and are exhausted in their enthusiasm for the Scriptures, when they wander in the desert and are not able to find the town. The Psalmist also mentions their madness too, saying, "they wandered in the wilderness in a solitary way; they found no city to dwell in."[23]

10:16/17. *Woe to you, O land, whose king acts as an adolescent, and whose ministers dine in the morning. Happy are you, O land, whose king is a man of dignity, and whose ministers dine at the proper time- in strength and not in drunkenness.* He seems in fact here to reprove the young king and to condemn indulgent judges, which in another place has been called wisdom that is weakened by age, and even in other places mature age which is made frail by pleasure. On the other hand he seems to approve the king with good morals, who is appointed easily. He also seems to praise those judges who nonetheless prefer pleasure to the business of the town, but after much toil and the running of the township, are forced to eat as if by necessity. But I find more holy what seems to lie hidden in the text, because those who depart from old laws and despise the precepts of their ageing fathers, are called young men in the scripture; they who do not heed the commandments of God, and desire to change the laws of mankind. The Lord of Israel threatens in Isaiah[24], because the people did not want the waters of Shiloah that flows in silence, and averted the ancient stream, choosing for themselves the rivers of Samaria, and the surges of Damascus. "And I will give", he says, "children to be their princes, and babes shall rule over them"[25]. Read also Daniel and you will find the old God of Days.[26] Or read the Apocalypse of John where the head of the Saviour is said to be white and snowy, and you will find it to be like white wool. Look at Jeremiah too because he was wise and his hair was purported to be white because of his wisdom, and he is forbidden to call himself a young man[27]. Woe to the land therefore whose king is the devil, who always desirous of new things, and even rebels against its parent in the case of Abessalon, who regards as judges and leaders those, who love the pleasures of the world, and who say before the day of death comes, "let us eat and drink, for tomorrow we die"[28]. For the other part is the blessed land of the Church whose king, Christ, is the son of all peoples. He is descended from Abraham and Isaac, and Jacob, also

24 Cfr. Is. 8, 1-
7.

25 Is. 3, 4.

26 Cfr. Dan. 7, 9
sqq.

27 Cfr. Ier. 1, 7.

28 Is. 22, 13.

85

from the stock of all the prophets and saints, for whom sin was not conquered. On account of this they were indeed children. Born of these was the virgin, more freely Saint Mary, who had no offspring, no seed from her flank, but all of her fruit burst out in flower, speaking in the Song of Songs: "I am the flower of the field and the lily of the valley"[29]. His leaders too are apostles and all are saintly, who see their king as the son of all men, the son of a free woman; not of the slave woman Agar, but born of Sara in freedom. And they do not eat in the morning, or quickly. For they do not seek enjoyment in their time, but eat in their time, and when the time for retribution will come, they will eat in strength, and not in disorder. Every good thing of this world is a disorder, but an everlasting strength in the future. Just this is said in Isaiah: "look at those who serve me, they will eat; but you will go hungry."[30] And again, "look at those who serve me, they will be happy; but you will shamed."[31]

29 Cant. 2, 1.

30 Is. 65, 13.

31 Is. 65, 14

10:18. Through *slothfulness the ceiling sags, and through idleness of the hands the house leaks.* Our house, which is held up by the condition of mankind, even that abode that we have in heaven, sags if we are lazy and slow to do good work. And every ceiling, which is supposed to hold the roof up high, falls to the ground and crushes its inhabitants. And when the help of hands and virtues has eventually gone numb a great storm of all tempests and rain clouds will fall down upon us from above. More precisely, although we have interpreted this with regard to one man, it can be better understood with bearing to the Church, because its stature is brought down by the neglect of its principate. There in the Church we find the attractions of sins, where the roof is said to be virtue.

10:19. A *feast is made for laughter, and wine gladdens life, but money answers everything.* I think that what follows relates to the preceding verses. For with regard to the sloth and the indolence of teachers the Church is lowered, and its roof is made to fall, and its timbers leak, as we have shown above. Therefore here he is speaking of the self-same teachers. And he has been seen to accuse them, asking why they remain silent and do not make use of their duty as teacher, (that is both for bishops and elders in the Church), saying that they neither work on their speaking nor doctrine, the same that even Titus admonishes[32], and is taught by Timothy[33], so that one does not forget the grace of God, which is bestowed upon a great man. But in this respect they see themselves as elders and bishops, so that they receive an allowance, and many teachers ask for

32 Cfr Tit. 1, 5.

33 Cfr. I Tim. 4, 14.

a two-fold glory, which is owed in fact to those who work on their speaking and doctrines. But now he takes the other side and accuses those who even speak in the Church and teach the congregation, but they teach the people that which they like to hear, because he flatters the sinner in his crime and incites the listeners to applaud. For surely when such a teacher is giving a lascivious speech in the Church, does he not promise the blessing and realm of heaven to the crowd, as it will seem to you that his laughter makes bread, and he mixes wine with the happiness of those who drink? Or as those who teach and seek riches, food, and wealth through the promised delights. Or the bread of the Church, which is the bread of mourners, and not of those who laugh, because those who weep are blessed, for they will laugh, and will have joy in their happiness. He also goes on to say: money or silver answers everything, and this must be taken as two-fold: either that those learned men become rich after their praise, and take their place at the head of the people, or indeed, since money is always taken in return for a speech: for "the words of the LORD are pure words: as silver extracted in a furnace of earth, purified seven times."[34] He asserts this because the ignoble crowd is always moved easily by eloquence and speeches, which are composed of a great foliage of words. Differently: those who have free-will and are forbidden to mourn and fast, make bread in their laughter. Isaac gets his name from this bread as well, and in the happiness of drinking they prepare wine. And so every holy man, who is teacher of the Church, as Christ commanded, makes bread in his laughter and happiness, and hands out cups of wine in his joy. Money also, which answers everything, is given out as five, and two and one talent for the head of the family in the Gospel[35]. And ten coins which are thought to be for slaves in business.

34 Ps. 12, 6.

35 Cfr. Matth. 25, 15-30.

10:20. Even *in your thoughts do not curse a king, and in your bed-chamber do not curse the rich, for a bird of the skies may carry the sound, and some winged creature may betray the matter.* This simple example teaches the listeners that we should not be overpowered by anger and fury, and curse and blame kings and leaders, since it seems to happen against one's wish, that what we curse is made known. And we run into danger by the inability to hold our tongue. He also says, "a bird of the skies may carry the sound, and some winged creature may betray the matter", this is to be understood as a exaggeration, just as we are accustomed to saying, 'walls have ears to hear those things, which we think are said in private'. But it is better to hear a teaching in this way, so that we know that we have a commandment to follow, not only that nothing should be spoken rashly against Christ, but also in the secret places of our heart, however we are troubled by our many problems, nothing should be blasphemed, nothing thought which is impious. And since we owe love, that we have for Christ, the next part says, "love the Lord your God," and even " your nearest" and "yourself".[36] He even orders this, so that afterwards we do not easily take the king away from the holy, and so that we do not slander by the wickedness of our tongue those who are rich in knowledge, wisdom and virtues, for they are the angels who fly around the earth and are administrators of the spirit. They say in Zechariah, "we have traversed the earth and look all the world is inhabited and quiet"[37]. And just like birds, our words and thoughts are carried to heaven. And whatever we think in secret, is not hidden from God's knowledge.

36 Matth. 22, 37.40.

37 Zach. 1, 11

Chapter 11

11:1. Send *your bread upon the waters, for after many days you will find it.* He encourages to mercy since it must be given to all that seek wisdom, and work well. For just as he sows over the well-watered fields and awaits the produce of his seed, so too he who is generous to the needy does not sow the grain of his seed, but bread itself. And he waits for it to grow into his future profit; and when the day of judgement comes much more will be found to have grown than was at first sown. Differently: in each and every man you can see this water, about which is said, "rivers flow from his stomach, the waters of life"[1], lest it should trouble you to display the bread of life, the bread of reasoning, and of speech. For if you do this many times you will find that you have not sown the seeds of doctrine in vain. I think that this is what is written in Isaiah too: "blessed is he who sows across the water, where the ox and ass trample"[2]. This is also because that teacher (about whom we have already spoken), is held to be worthy of blessing, because he sows across the well-watered hearts of his listeners, the hearts of the Jews, as those of the gentiles in the gathered congregation.

11:2. Give *a portion to seven, and also to eight; for you do not know what evil shall be upon the earth.* And in Ezekiel there are found seven or eight steps leading up to the temple.[3] And after the 'ethical' Psalm, that is one hundred and eighteen, all the psalms are of fifteen steps by which we are first taught the law, and when the seventh is finished, we then climb to the Gospel through the 'eight steps'[4]. Therefore it is taught that we should believe with equal respect in each, the same for the old as for the new. The Jews dedicated their seventh part, believing in the Sabbath, but did not dedicate that eighth, denying the resurrection on the day of the Lord. On the other hand, heretics, Marcion and Manichaeus and all who rip up the ancient law with their savage mouths, dedicate their eighth part, taking up the Gospel. But they do not save as holy the seventh, spurning the old law. For we are not able to understand the worthy crucifixions, the worthy punishments already in mind, which are reserved for those who are moved to wickedness on earth, that is for the Jews and the heretics, and for those denying the other of the two. The Hebrews understand this passage in this way: keep both the Sabbath and the rite of circumcision, for if you do not adhere to these wickedness will come over you unexpectedly.

1 Ioh. 7, 38.

2 Is. 32, 20.

3 Ez. 40, 26.31.

4 Ier. 'ogdoadem'

11:3. **If** *the clouds are full of rain, they empty themselves upon the earth: and if the tree falls toward the south, or toward the north, in the place where the tree falls, there it shall be.* Keep the commandments that have been taught to you above so that the clouds above you will break open in rain. For wherever you have made your home and seat for the future, whether to the east or facing the north, when you die you will remain there. Differently: as I have said above 'send your bread over the water and divide it to all who ask'. Since when the clouds are full they pour their riches down on mortals, and you are as a tree: however aged you may be, you will not live forever, but one day suddenly struck by the storm of death like a storm of winds, there where you fall you will lie forever. The time of your end will come whether you may be stiff and savage, or mild and merciful. Differently: God is addressed in the Psalms: "you are truth up to the clouds"[5], and in Isaiah God warns the sinner of the vineyard, "I will command the clouds not to rain down"[6]. Therefore the clouds are as prophets or holy men, who have amassed many talents in their mind, so that he can rain his teachings of doctrine down on others and say, "their speech should be awaited just as rain, and they will pour out rain across the earth"[7], to which is replied, "let the earth hear the words of my mouth"[8]. But this follows: "and if a tree falls to the east, or to the north, in the place where it falls, there it will remain." We can take the example of the book of Hebrews, in which is written, "God will come to Teyma"[9], which some interpreters have taken to mean that God will come from the south, and when I come to think about it the south is always used in a good context. This can be seen in Song of Songs: "arise oh north" that is 'return' and 'go away'; "and come O south wind"[10]. Therefore a tree, if in this life it falls and is cut in its state of mortality, either must sin before while it stands and is then placed in the north afterwards, or if the south winds takes away all its worthy fruit, it will lie wounded in the south. The text does not mean any tree, but only if it lies to the north or south. This means the same as that which is written: "I will say to the north wind, come, and to the south wind, do not hold back"[11]. Nowhere teaches about the south wind and the east wind together, saying that they blow, since it is fitting for them to be among those regions, because they are blown afterwards to the south and east. Therefore it

5 Ps. 35, 6.

6 Is. 5, 6.

7 Deut. 32, 2.

8 Deut. 32, 1.

9 Heb. 3,3.

10 Cant. 4, 16.

11 Is. 43, 6

90

blows from the north to the south and the south wind blows its inhabitants to the east. And they are not able to blow out if they remain in their ancient palaces.

11:4. He *that observes the wind shall not sow; and he that regards the clouds shall not reap.* He who considers what is good for him and does not give out to all who ask him, often destroys what he ought to receive.[12] Differently: he who proclaims the word of God at the time when the people listen freely and a second wind of rumour comes, he is a negligent and lazy farmer. But favourably or not in his career he must proclaim the word of God[13]; and he must not think of the storm of adverse clouds in his time of faith. This is written in Proverbs: "just as the rains are heavy and unyielding, so are they who leave wisdom and praise impiety"[14]. Therefore you must sow your seeds in the middle of a storm without thinking of the clouds and without fearing the winds. And you must not say, 'that time was convenient, this of no use', when we do not know which way and which will is the one spirit of giving.

11:5 As *you do not know what is the way of the spirit, nor how the bones do grow in the womb of her that is with child: even so you know not the works of God who makes all.* Just as you do not know the way of the spirit and of the soul entering a child, and are unknowing of the types of bone and veins in the stomach of a pregnant woman. It is hard to know how the human body is formed from the simplest elements into the many varied forms and limbs, and from the very same seed, one makes soft our hair, another makes our bones hard; one connects the veins, another links the nerves together. Thus you cannot know the work of God, who has made all things. From this he teaches that the variety of things in the world must not be feared, and you must not fear the winds and the clouds, which as we have mentioned above must be judged. But although the sower ought to reap in the course of his career, he ought to save the outcome for the judgement of the Lord.

11:6/8. *In the morning sow your seed, and in the evening withhold not your hand: for you know not whether shall prosper, either this or that, or whether they both shall be alike good. Truly the light is sweet, and a pleasant thing it is for the eyes to behold the sun: But if a man lives many years, and rejoices in them all; yet let him remember the days of darkness; for they shall be many. All that which comes is vanity.* Do not choose which good deeds

12 Cfr. Luc 6, 30.

13 Cfr II Tim. 4, 2.

14 Prov. 28, 3.4

you do, but once you have started doing good, never stop. The evening will reveal the justice of the morning, and the sunrise will collect the mercy of the evening. For it is uncertain which work pleases God more, and by what means you will obtain the fruit of righteousness. But it can happen that not one but each one will please God. Another meaning could be that both in childhood and in old-age you will have equal work. Do not say therefore, "I worked while I was able, I ought to rest in old-age", for you do not know whether you please God more in youth or in age. And the thrift of youth too is of no use if old-age is taken up by indulgence. For the righteous has erred, not even his former virtues can free him from death. And if you always do well according to each interpretation and work equal amounts in each age, you will see God the Father, the sweetest light; you will see Christ, the sun of righteousness. More precisely if you live for many years and always have good things or do good deeds, you will still know that you are going to die, and the coming of darkness will continually surround you: you will despise the present things as if they were transient, frail and failing. Symmachus has interpreted the end of this idea in this way: if a man lives for many years and if he has been happy in all this he ought to remember the days of darkness, since they will be many, in which all will cease. Differently: in another place in the Scripture God promises, saying, "I will give you timely rain and rain that is late"[15]. I will irrigate you with rain: the Old and the New Testament. He warns about this here so that we may read about the ancient law, lest we hate the Gospel, and in this way ask about the spiritual understanding in the old text; lest we think that what we read in the Gospels and apostles is only to be taken at face value. For we do not know when more knowledge and grace is divested to us by God, and he who is happy, who joined both together to make it like one. For he who has followed this will see the light, will see Christ, the light of justice. And if he lives for several years and with knowledge of the Scriptures he will know the greatest happiness and enjoyment, and he is forced more to this toil by the memory of his future judgement. Since the time of eternal darkness will come, and perpetual punishments will be in stone for those who have not sown in the morning and in the evening, and joined both in vain; they have not seen the light or the sun, whence the light itself comes.

15 Deut. 11, 14.

11:9/10. *Rejoice, O young man, in your youth; and let your heart cheer you in the days of your youth, and walk in the ways of your* *heart, and in the sight of your eyes: but know, that for all these things God will bring you into judgement. Therefore remove sorrow from your heart, and put away evil from your flesh: for childhood and youth are vanity.*

Chapter 12

12:1 Remember *now your Creator in the days of your youth, while the evil days come not, nor the years draw nigh, when you shall say, I have no pleasure in them;* In this chapter there were many explanations of all things and almost as many opinions as men themselves. It would take too long however to recount all the opinions of everyone and their arguments in which they want to prove their opinions, the matter would require a volume to itself. But it is enough for wise men to have shown what they feel, and like in a small picture, to have depicted the thirst of the earth, the waste of the whole earth, and the belt of the ocean, and to have shown them in such a small collection. The Hebrews believe the imperative here refers to Israel, to whom it is taught that she should enjoy her riches, and before the time of bondage comes should change youth to old-age. She should enjoy whatever is pleasant or fun, just as it seems to the heart so it seems to the eyes; at that time while she still has them to hand. She knows however that she will be judged in all things that she has done. And just as from bad thoughts she flees from desires, knowing that foolishness is joined to youth, and will remember always her Creator, and before the days of Babylonian and Roman captivity come, in which she will no longer be free. And all of this passage from the point which says, "before the sun, moon, and stars become dark"[1], until the place where the Scripture reminds us, "and dust will be swirled on earth just as it used to be and the soul returned to God who gave it"[2], they explain their condition. And since as I have said above these things are tiresome and favourable, they should be touched by us but briefly and superficially. Therefore enjoy your youth O Israel, and do this or that, that has already been mentioned before your time of bondage comes; and your glory will leave you and pride, and judges, and your holy men who want to be interpreted as the sun, moon, and stars, and are taken away. Before Nebuchadnezzar comes, or Titus, Vespasian's son, before the call of the prophets and their prophecies are fulfilled. In that day when the angels that protect the temple leave, and the strongest men in your army are thrown in confusion, and the speeches of the judges will be slow to come, and the prophets, who are accustomed to receiving the light of their visions from heaven, they all will become dark. When the doors of the temple are closed Jerusalem will be made humble and the Chaldeans will come as if by the song of a bird, called thus in the words of Jeremiah, and the singing girls with the lute in the temple choir will become silent[3]. At that time, when they will come to Jerusalem,

1 Eccl. 12, 2.

2 Eccl. 12, 7.

3 Cfr Ier. 9.

94

4 Cfr Is. 37

5 Cfr Ier. 1, 11.

the enemies too will fear the greatness of God, and in the way of doubt, they will fear the death of Sennacherib. For they also believe the saying, "and from up high they will fear and tremble in the road"[4]. In those days "the almond tree will flourish", that stick and staff which Jeremiah saw in his prophecy in the beginning, "and the grasshopper will be a burden"[5]. Nebuchadnezzar with his army, "and desire shall fail ", the friendship between Israel and God. But what desire wants for itself, although we have begun to speak about them individually will be explained more fully. But all this will happen to Israel, because man will go out into the house of his eternity, and having returned from the protection of God to the heavens, going to his tabernacle, the weeping and crying will wander in the street and will be hemmed in by the enemy's siege. Be happy therefore Israel in your youth, before the silver cord is broken, (this is until your glory is with you), before the golden ribbon breaks off, (that is before the arc of the tabernacle is taken away); before the pitcher is worn away to the fountain, and the wheel is turned around over the pool. That is until you read the most sacred teachings, for the spirit of a holy man is grace, and before you return to Babylon, from whence you left the loins of Abraham, and you will begin to be worn away in Mesopotamia, which once breathed life into you, and all is returned to He who gave it. The Jews have always taught these things and have understood this chapter to pertain to themselves. But I prefer to return to the previous argument, and try to explain each thing individually: "rejoice O youth, in your adolescence, and let your heart be good in the days of your youth, and walk in the way of your heart and in the sight of your eyes; and know above all these things, since God will lead you into judgement". He has said that the light of this world is the sweetest and that man ought to rejoice in the days of his life, and grasp desire with all enthusiasm. For the eternal night of death will fall when it's not permitted to enjoy ones amassed wealth and like a shadow, all things that we possess, will die. Now therefore he encourages man and says, "O youth, before old-age and death fall upon you, enjoy your youth, and whatever you feel is good, and seems joyful to see, take it and enjoy as it please you the things of this world." Again so that he does not think these things say to provoke men to indulgence, and thus fall into the doctrines of Epicurus, he takes this suspicion, saying, "and know, since above all these God will lead you to judgement". Thus, he says, take advantage of the things of the world, so that you know you will be judged in the end. "And force anger from your heart and take wickedness from your flesh, since youth and foolishness

95

are vanity". In anger he sees all the problems of the spirit. In the wickedness of the flesh he sees every desire of the body. In this way therefore, he says, enjoy the goodness of this world, lest you leave pleasure or flesh. Leave off your former vices, which you did in your youth of vanity and foolishness, since youth is joined to foolishness. "And remember in the day of your youth Him, who created you, before the days of wickedness come and the years approach, in which you will say, 'I have no will'". Always remember your Creator and walk the route of your youth, so that you remember your end is death, before your time comes, in which sad things will happen.

12:2 While *the sun, or the light, or the moon, or the stars, be not darkened, nor the clouds return after the rain.* If we take this from the creation of the world, this chapter agrees with the words of the Lord, in which He says, "there will be trouble and difficulty as there has not been since the beginning of creation, but this will not happen. For the sun will grow dark and the moon will not shed light, and the stars will fall from the sky, and the virtues of heaven will be moved"[6]. Those things are the guardians of the house, as we understand the 'house' to be this world, and the strong men, deceived by wickedness and varied strengths must be dispersed. But if a particular consummation of any one person is kept to the end of his life, then the sun, the moon, and stars, clouds and rain will cease to be for him, who has died. Differently: enjoy youth, O Christian people, and enjoy the goodness which has been given to you by God, and know that God will judge you for all these. Do not think that, since the earlier branches have been broken, you will be placed in the root of a good olive tree, and therefore you will be without worry. But remove anger from your heart and desires from your body, and when you have left all other vices remember your Creator before the day of wickedness comes, the day of madness, in which punishments have been made for sinners. This is so that when you sin the sun of righteousness will set for you at midday, and the light of knowledge will die, and the brightness of the moon, (that is of the Church) will be taken away, and the stars will die, about which is written, "in which you shine like the lights in the world having reason of life"[7]. And elsewhere: "star differs from star in glory. Before the clouds return after the rain"[8], lest the prophets, who have watered the hearts of believers by the rain of their speech, after they have seen you to be

6 Matth. 24, 21.19.

7 Phil. 2, 15.

8 I Cor. 15, 41

96

unworthy of their rain, return to their seat, clearly to Him from whom they were sent.

12:3 *In the day when the keepers of the house shall tremble, and the strong men shall bow themselves;* The keepers of the house can be interpreted as either the sun and the moon, and the remaining choir of stars, or the angels who keep watch over this world. The men of great strength though, or the brave, as Symmachus has interpreted it, are those who die, or as Aquila has translated it, those who err, and are felt to be demons, for they are called those chosen by the powerful devil. The Lord overpowered him, and joining him, according to the parable of the Gospel[9], destroys his house. Differently: the keepers of the house, who relate all things, which are written to the body of man, think that it means ribs, because the intestines are hemmed in by them, and all of the fleshy parts of the stomach are protected in this way. They think that the strong men are to be interpreted as legs; the sun and moon and stars therefore pertain to the eyes, nose and ears, and receive all the sensations of the head. But they do not interpret this to such an extent, because they are forced deeper by necessity, not by demons, or the sun, moon, or stars, but to understand what follows according to the limbs of man. *And the grinders cease because they are few, and those that look out of the windows be darkened.* In the beginning of the world when the charity of most was cold and the spirits of teachers were few, who were able to offer the food of heaven to believers, and they were carried to the heaves; then those who in part see the light of knowledge in this world began to be darkened. For it is said to Moses: "sit yourself in this hole in the rock, and you will see me pass"[10]. Oh how much more one spirit saw the truth through that opening and those dark caves! Differently: there are two grinders, from whom one is taken, the other is left, the Gospel is not silent in this matter[11]. And when they are few, and have ceased, it is necessary that every light of knowledge is removed from our eyes. Differently: they think the grinders have ceased because they are few, and that it is talking about teeth. And when at last old-age comes even teeth are worn away, or they fall out, which usually grind down food to be sent to the stomach. But seeing it grow dark in the caves, they think it means eyes because sight darkens with old-age, and sight is made difficult.

12:4 *And the doors shall be shut in the streets, when the sound of the grinding is low, and he shall rise up at the voice of the bird,*

9 Luc. 11, 14-26.

10 Ex. 33, 22.

11 Cfr. Matth. 24, 41.

12 Cfr. Matth.
25, 1-12.

and all the daughters of music shall be brought low. When the voice of the grinder is weak and the teaching of a tutor has stopped, then in turn all things will stop. Even the doors are closed in the streets, as according to the unwieldy virgins of the Gospel[12], and each one regards her doors as closed to her in the street, so that she can not buy oil. Or even, while the virgins are wandering in the streets, husbands close each room when they have entered into it. For if the road is thin and narrow, which leads to life and that

13 Cfr. Matth. 7,
13

which leads to death is wide and open, justly, the charity of most being cold, the door of teachings is closed in the streets.[13] But let us use the following verse, in which he says, "and he rises to the sound of a bird", (or of a sparrow), if we seem to be a sinner to the voice of the bishop or elder so to show that we are in repentance. But this could also be different again, if we do not follow the context of this chapter, it can be taken to mean the real resurrection, when the death will rise up to the voice of the arch-angel. And it is not surprising, if we compare the trumpet of an angel to a sparrow, when all night is compared to Christ, if it is clement. And also this is not too surprising, if my memory serves

14 Ps. 10, 1.

15 Ps. 101, 8.

16 Ps. 83, 4.

me right, when I have never read of a sparrow in a bad light. In the tenth Psalm a righteous man says, "I trust in God, just as you say to my spirit: fly to the mountain like a sparrow."[14] And in another place: "I woke and I was made as a sparrow alone on a roof"[15]. Nor is it seen in a bad light in another place: "and even the sparrow found a home for himself"[16]. Differently: they want to see this as the closed doors in the street, as the weak steps of an old man, because he always sits and cannot walk. The weakness of the voice of the grinder is interpreted as in his jaws, because he cannot chew food, and scarcely reduced in spirit, his voice is heard only quietly. More precisely he shows him to rise to the sound of a bird, because now with cold blood and dry organs by which sleep is nourished, he wakes to a soft sound, and in the middle of the night, when the cock crows, he rises quickly; but he is not able to move his limbs from his bed. And he becomes silent too, or as it is better put in the Hebrew, the daughters of song become deaf, (meaning ears), because it is harder for old-men to hear noises and there is less distinction between voices, or enjoy songs. Also compare what Berzellai says to David, when he does not want to go to Jordan.[17]

17 Cfr. II reg.
19, 32-39.

12:5.*Also when they shall be afraid of that which is high, and fears shall be in the way.* That is, they will not be able to enter on difficult tasks and with tired knees and frightened footsteps, will not be able to go out in the open, and will fear the offence of steps. *And*

98

the almond tree shall flourish, and the grasshopper shall be a burden, and desire shall fail: because man goes to his long home, and the mourners go about the streets. The speech now explains the limbs of a man of the Church through a metaphor. And when old-age comes his hair will grow white, his feet will swell, his lust will grow cold and he will be destroyed by death. Then he will be returned to the earth, and then in the house of his eternity you will remember his tomb and his ashes with reverence, and a crowd will walk before the mourners at his funeral. But the flower of the almond-tree, which we have in place of grey hairs, some interpret as the sacred thorn, because, while the flesh of the buttocks decreases, the thorn grows and flowers. More precisely, in that verse which says, "the grasshopper will be a burden", you must note that where we have in our manuscripts 'grasshopper', the Hebrew has *aagab*, which is rather ambiguous for us. For it can be translated as 'heel' or as 'grasshopper'. Just as for example in the beginning of Jeremiah, the word *soced* if the accent is changed can mean 'a nut' or 'wakefulness'. And this is said to him: "what do you see, Jeremiah?" and he replies, "a nut".[18] And the Lord says to him, "you have seen well, for I will wake over my work so that I might complete it."[19] Or that explanation: it also has the etymology of the word 'nut', because God is about to keep awake. And what the people has deserved it will be given, is what the text seems to say. Thus now he shows the ambiguity of the word through its etymology, showing that the legs of old men swell up and that gout weighs upon the organs. This does not happen to all men, but to most, and this is *synecdoche* where a part is called by the name of the whole. Indeed where we read 'desire' the Hebrew has *abiona*. This in itself has many meanings, and is interpreted as 'love', 'lust', 'longing', or 'desire'. And it has the meaning, as I have said above, that the lust of an old man grows cold, and the organs of intercourse sag. But this is said because these words are ambiguous, for although they mean 'almond-tree', and 'grasshopper', and 'desire' in his language, they also mean other derived words in our language, and are derived from the forms which pertain to old-age. You must note too, that where the Septuagint has the word 'almond-tree' the word itself is *soced*, which is found in the beginning of Jeremiah. But there it is meant 'nut' but here it means 'almond-tree'. Symmachus has interpreted this passage in a greatly different way, (though I am unsure of what he means): for he says, 'and they will see even above these things from on high, and they will wander, and waking he will fall asleep, and the strength of his spirit will be dispersed.' For man will go to

18 Ier. 1, 11.

19 Ier. 1, 12

99

the house of his eternity, and the weeping will wander in the street. Laodicenus[20] followed the interpretation of Symmachus, which the Hebrews do not like, nor the Christians; for while he is far from the Hebrews' view, he rejects too the interpretations of the Septuagint.

20 Apollinaris Laodic

12:6/8. *Or ever the silver cord be loosed, or the golden bowl be broken, or the pitcher be broken at the fountain, or the wheel broken at the cistern. Then shall the dust return to the earth as it was: and the spirit shall return unto God who gave it. Vanity of vanities says Ecclesiastes; all is vanity.* He returns to former matter and after a rather large exaggeration, -which he interposes in this place, in which he says, "and remember your Creator, in the day of your youth; before the days of wickedness come, and before the sun, moon grow dark" and so on, "in the day in which the keepers of the house are renewed". - now he finishes the point he had begun in a similar way, saying, "before the silver cord is broken", and this or that happens. But he shows the silver cord to be this white band, and the space that divides us from heaven. It also means the gold band, which returns to the place whence it came down. more precisely the two that follow, the wearing of the jug on the fountain, and the breaking of the wheel by the pond, are metaphorical images of death. For death is just like the jug, which is worn down, stops to fill, and the wheel by which water is carried from a well or pond, if it has been broken. Thus the interpretation of the Septuagint has it that the usage of water is twisted in this rope; thus when the silver cord is broken, and the river of the spirit flows back to the fountain, the man will die. He goes on more clearly: "the dust will return to the earth, whence it was taken, and the spirit is returned to God, who gave it". From which there is enough to smile at in those who think that spirits are produced with bodies, not from God, but are made from the parent's body. For when the flesh is returned to the earth, and the spirit goes back to God, who gave it; it is obvious that God is the parent of all spirits, not man. Then after the description of man's death, he goes back to the beginning of his book, saying, "vanity of vanities, says Ecclesiastes, all is vanity"[21]. For all toil of mortal men, which is

21 Eccl. 1,2.

argued all through the books, is pertinent here, so that dust returns to the earth, and the spirit returns to the place, whence it was taken, it is a great vanity in this world to toil and obtain nothing for the future from it.

12:9/10. *And moreover, because the preacher was wise, he still taught the people knowledge; yea, he gave good heed, and sought out, and set in order many proverbs. The preacher sought to find out acceptable words: and that which was written was upright, even words of truth.* The wisdom in which Solomon judges all kinds of men he now professes at the end, because he was not happy with the use of the old law, but therefore immersed himself in trying to solve difficult problems of his own accord, and in teaching people; he composed parables and proverbs, which say one thing superficially and yet have a deeper meaning. For proverbs often have different meaning to that which is written, and this is the method used in teaching in the Gospels, since the Lord spoke to the people in parables and in proverbs[22], but He explained them to the apostles in secret. From this we clearly get the Book of Proverbs, and we shouldn't think that they are but simple stories with teachings, but rather as gold still in the earth, as a seed within a nut, or as a fruit is found inside the hairy covering of its peel. Thus we must search for another meaning in them which pertains to God. Before this though he mentions that he desired to know the workings of the world and the wisdom and mind of God. He wanted to know why one thing or another should happen, as David after the death of the body and spirit hoped he would see the path to heaven, saying, "I will see the heavens, the work of your fingers"[23]. But now Solomon strives to find this wisdom, so that he may know and understand with his human mind, though confined by the walls of the body, the truth only known by God.

12:11 The *words of the wise are as goads, and as nails fastened by the masters of assemblies, which are given from one shepherd.* The teacher should not be seen to break from the law of God and afterwards to justify teaching by himself, more hastily than Moses not so much of his own will, as first by the anger of God, took teachings therefrom with enthusiasm. He says that his words are the words of the wise, which like a goad correct the wicked and they move the slow steps of mortals with a sharp sting, thus they are hard like nails which hold things up securely and high; and they are not offered with one man's authority, but with the advice and agreement of all teachers. Let not mankind's wisdom be despised, for he says it is given from one shepherd. That is, many are allowed to teach, but there is only one originator of the teachings, who is God. He turns the passage against those who think there is one God of the Old Law, and one God of the Gospels, since one shepherd taught the advice of the

22 Cfr. Matth, 13; 15.

23 Ps. 8, 4

wise. But the wise are just as much prophets as the apostles themselves. At the same time it should be remembered that the words of the wise are said to sting, not to flatter or encourage debauchery by a lack of discipline. But as I have said above it is to give the wound and slow pain of repentance to those who have come into wickedness. For if his speech does not sting but it like pleasure for the listeners then that is not the speech of a wise man. For the words of the wise are like the goad, since after all they cause the conversion of the wicked, are firm, given on the advice of saints, given by the one shepherd, and are founded on a strong root. I think I have heard it said in Paul that Saul was thrown into the way of wickedness by this goad: "it is hard for you to kick against the pricks."[24]

12:12 And *further, by these, my son, be admonished: of making many books there is no end; and much study is a weariness of the flesh.* If you remove the words which are given by the one shepherd, related by the advice and agreement of the wise, do nothing and nothing will be reproved you; follow in the footsteps of the multitude and do not diverge from their command. Then too for him who seeks to know many things there is a great number of books that will lead him to wickedness and make the reader toil in vain. But he also teaches that you must have enthusiasm and follow meanings more than the words themselves, the opposite that philosophers and teachers of this world teach, who try to assert the falsities of their doctrines with flamboyant and unnecessary language. On the other hand divine scripture is restricted by the small quantity of what is written, and however much it is enlarged by people's opinions it is restricted by the text itself. This is because the Lord has made speech concise and brief all over the world, and His word is the same when it is spoken in our mouth and our heart.[25] Differently: read often, then consider what you have read daily, there is usually more toil of the mind that that of the body. For just as whatever you do with your hand and body is filled with the toil of the hand and the body, so that which pertains to reading is more the toil of the mind. It seems to me from this that the above points from the several books must be considered differently to the way in which many believe them to be. It is the custom of the Scriptures that, no matter how many books there are, if they all follow the same matter are have few differences, then we can say that they are one book. In this way the Gospel and the "immaculate law of the Lord, converting spirits"[26] are called one, although there are several books in the Gospel and there are many

24 Act. 9, 5.

25 Cfr. Deut. 30, 14; Rom. 10, 8.

26 Ps. 18, 8

27 Cfr. Ez. 3, 1-3.

28 Cfr. Apoc. 10, 9.

29 Ps. 39, 9.

30 Cfr. Ioh. 1, 2.

31 Prov. 10, 19.

32 I Cor. 15, 10.

33 Ps. 68, 4

laws. In this way too there is one volume of Isaiah, and all of the divine Scripture has one title; Ezekiel[27] and John[28] are also many books in one book. The Saviour too prophesied in the holy words, saying, "in the title of the Book is written about me"[29]. According to this meaning therefore I think it is a teaching that there should not be too many books. For whatever you say, if it is told to him who was with God in the beginning, the word then is God[30], as one volume, and the many books are the one law, which is called the Gospel. But if you argue that they are varied and differ too much to be in the same volume, and look at them with too much curiosity, even within each book you will see that there are many books. They say about this: "you may not escape the sin of saying too much"[31]. Therefore there is no end to such books, for all is good and the ending locks in truth, but wickedness and lying have no end. And the more they are sought, the more they come about. Study and consideration of this is toil of the body. I say of the body here and not of the spirit. But the spirit even has toil according to what the apostle says: "the more I worked for all these, not I, but the grace of God which was with me"[32], and the Saviour says, "I worked shouting"[33].

12:13/14. *Let us hear the conclusion of the whole matter: Fear God, and keep his commandments: for this is the whole duty of man. For God shall bring every work into judgement, with every secret thing, whether it be good, or whether it be evil.* The Hebrews say that although it used to be among other writings of Solomon in the past, they have not persisted in memory; and this book seems as if it ought to have been omitted, because it asserts that all God's creations are vain and that he thinks everything is done for nothing, and he prefers food and drink and transient pleasures to all things; thus he takes his authority from this one title, so it is now included in the number of divine books, because he argues well and lists many things like *anakephaiosei,* and he said that his speeches are the easiest to hear, and to understand; let us therefore fear God and carry out his commandments. For man is born for this purpose and, understanding his Creator, he reveres Him in fear and respect, and in the work of his commandments. And when the time of judgement comes whatever we have done will stand before the judge and for a long time we will await our judgement which could go one way or the other, and we will receive our just rewards, whether they be good or bad. But where we read, "with every secret thing", Symmachus and the Septuagint have interpreted, "from all contempt", or even "from all unknown", which even brought by

103

reluctant words, not by will, but by ignorance, we will be returned to reason in the day of our judgement. Differently: since fear is more appropriate to slaves, and perfect love involves no fear, and fear in the divine Scripture is used to denote those embarking on and those completing education[34]. Now I think he talks about the fear inherent in virtues, according to the passage, which says, "nothing is lacking from those who fear Him"[35]. Or even, since until now he is a man and has not yet taken the name of God, he has this reason of his wealth, so that he fears God while he is still alive. Since every single deed is judged, that is, God leads all men into judgement about all things, either good or bad, which are done and said differently than by Him. For indeed, "woe to those who say wicked is good, and good is wicked"[36].

34 Cfr. I. Ioh. 4, 18.

35 Ps. 33, 10.

36 Is. 5, 20.

Translation Notes

1.   The term 'interpretes Septuaginta' has been translated simply as 'The Septuagint' though it should be more rightly 'the seventy translators' according to the Latin. By doing this I have taken into account capitalisation of the 's' and modern convention.

2.   The Latin word 'Saluator' has been translated throughout as 'the Saviour'.

3.   The Latin 'Dominus' has been translated as 'Lord' throughout in accordance with the King James Version. Thus 'deus' has simply been translated as 'God'.

4.   Jerome's transliteration of the Hebrew text is sometimes not in accordance with modern received pointing. This is because he worked in all probability from a text without pointing. Therefore in such cases as the commentary on I. 13. He takes the word now known as 'inyan' as 'anian'. cf. Usage at I. 14. ; II. 2. Transliteration of the furtive patah is reversed: in VI. 9. 'ruah' [wind] is written 'ruha'.

5.   Occurrences of Greek words in the text have for the most part not been translated in an attempt to preserve the original multilingual feel of the text. In the majority of cases Jerome himself translates the meaning.

6.   In some passages the commentary is lacking, such as for the text of VI. 11, but this is because Jerome clearly felt the passage to be self-explanatory or that he had already explained the meaning in a previous or following commentary.

7.   In book seven the Latin text is misaligned from the King James Version, while VII.1 in Jerome corresponds to VI. 12. In the KJV. This discrepancy is retained throughout this chapter but not further.

8.   In translating the Latin I have tried to retain the talkative and sometimes awkward style of the text as it stands. Though well written, many passages are difficult to translate as Jerome often makes mental jumps from one topic to another without clear explanation. I have therefore tried to preserve this original feeling in the text without making the translation unintelligible to the English-speaking reader.

Robin MacGregor 3/1/2000

COMMENTARY ON JONAH

Saint Jerome

Translated by

Robin MacGregor

PREFACE

This version of Jerome's Commentary on the Book of Jonah is a literal rendering of the original Latin text as set out in the Corpus Christianorum. As is usual in Jerome's commentaries he points out that he has tried to translate from the Hebrew and return to the original meanings, still a novel intention at the time of composition, and to compare this with the Greek version of Symmachus. I have therefore tried to maintain the multilingual feel of the original Latin in preserving the original Greek words in the text, though for the most part Jerome himself translates the meaning of these.

The editorial and Scriptural notes of the CCL have been preserved in this volume, as they are often very useful in enlightening Jerome's wide use of Scriptural quotation and reference. As it stands the text as set out in the CCL seems to be very secure and without cause for concern. Where seemed appropriate however a different reading taken from the other available editions has been used in order to preserve what is a more suitable or likely rendition of the original meaning.

For the most part I have tried to keep to the text of the King James Version in translating Jerome's text of Ecclesiastes but where this has differed from his Vulgate edition I have always taken the latter and translated his original Latin rather than keeping to the modern text. Preference has therefore always been given to a correct rendition of the original text and commentary together.

Robin MacGregor

7th February 2000

PROLOGUE

About three years have now passed since I first started writing the commentaries on the five Prophets, Micah, Nahum, Habakkuk, Zephaniah, and Haggai. Detained by another work, I was not able to finish what I had undertaken. For I was writing a book on famous men and two volumes against Jovinian, an apology and an essay on 'the best way to translate', which was addressed to Pammachius, two books to or about Nepotian, and other works which it would be lengthy to recount. Therefore I retake up my commentaries with Jonah after such a long absence. Jonah, a type of Savior, who prefiguring the resurrection of the Lord by spending *three days and three nights in the belly of a whale* (Mt. 12:40), was able to attain the first ardor so that we might deserve the arrival of the Holy Spirit to us. If indeed Jonah is to be translated as 'dove', and if the dove can be seen as the Holy Spirit, then we can also interpret the Dove as signifying the dove's entrance into us. I know that some classical authors, both Latin and Greek, have spoken much about this book, and through all of their questions have less enlightened than obscured the ideas, so that in effect their interpretation needs to be interpreted and with the result that the reader comes away feeling less sure of the meaning than beforehand. I am not saying this to criticize these great minds, to abase others in order to extol myself, but rather because it is the place of the commentator to clarify in short and clearly what is obscure; they should be less concerned with displaying their eloquence than with explaining the meaning of the author. We ask therefore where else the prophet Jonah appears in the Holy Scriptures apart from this book and the allusion made to him by the Lord in the Gospels (Mt. 12:39;Lk. 11:30). And if I am not mistaken he is mentioned in the book of Kings in this way: *in the fifth year of Amasiah, the son of Joash, King of Judah, began to rule the son of Jeroboam son of Joash King of Israel in Samaria, for forty-one years. He did much wickedness before the Lord and did not distance himself from all the sins of Jeroboam, son of Nebat, who caused Israel to sin. He re-established the frontier of Israel in Samaria from the entrance of Emathia to the Sea of Solitude, according to the word of the Lord God of Israel, which was spoken by the mouth of his servant Jonah, son of Amittai the prophet, from Gath which is in Ofer* (2 Kgs. 14:23-25). The Hebrews recount that he was the son of the widow of Sarepta,

109

incited by the prophet Elijah; his mother later said to him, *I know now that you are indeed a man of God, and that the word of God is truly in your mouth* (1 Kgs. 17:24); on account of this the child was called Truth. For Amittai in Hebrew can be rendered 'truth' in our language, and because Elijah spoke true, he who was encouraged was called the son of Truth. And Gath is located two miles from Sepphoris which is now called Diocaesarea, when you are travelling to Tiberia: there is a small castle where his tomb can be seen. Others, however, prefer to place his birth and tomb near Diospolis, which is in Lydia. They do not see that when he writes 'Ofer', this is to distinguish Gath from other towns of this name that can be seen now near to Eleutheropolis or Diospolis. The book of Tobit, though not in the canon, is all the same used by the men of the Church, also mentions Jonah when Tobit says to his son, *my son, I am old and ready to leave this life. Take your sons and go to Media, my son. For I know what the prophet Jonah has said about Nineveh: she will be destroyed* (Tob. 14:3). And, indeed, according to the Hebrew and Greek historians, Herodotus in particular, we read that Nineveh was destroyed in the time of King Josiah according to the Hebrews, and King Astyage of the Medians. From this we understand that in the past Jonah predicted that the Ninivites would repent and seek pardon; but afterwards, as they persisted in their sins, they brought the judgment of God upon themselves. The Hebrew tradition is that Hosea, Amos, Isaiah and Jonah prophesied at the same time. This is historical tradition. Not forgetting the others of course: the venerable Pope Chromatius, who took great pains to recount to the Savior the story of the prophet: he flees, he sleeps, he is thrown into the sea, he is swallowed by a whale, thrown back onto the shore and prays for repentance. And saddened by the safety of this town of many people, he finds comfort in the shade of a fig tree. There he is reproached by God for having taken more care of a green vine which had dried up, than of such a great number of men, and the other details I will try to explain in this volume. But to grasp the complete meaning of the prophet in this short preface there is no better interpretation than that which inspired the prophets and which marked out the lines of the truth of the future for its servants. He therefore speaks to the Jews who do not believe his words and are ignorant of Christ, the son of God: *the men of Nineveh will rise up at the time of judgment with that generation and they will condemn it, for they repented as Jonah*

110

required, and here there is more than Jonah! (Mt. 12:41). The generation of the Jews is condemned, while the world has faith and Nineveh repents, Israel the disbeliever dies. The Jews have the books themselves, we have the Lord of books; they hold the prophets, we have an understanding of the prophets; "the letter kills them", *the spirit makes us live* (2 Cor. 3:6); with them Barabbas the robber is released, for us Christ the Son of God is freed.

CHAPTER 1

1:1-2 *Now the word of the LORD came unto Jonah the son of Amittai, saying, Arise, go to Nineveh, that great city, and cry against it; for their wickedness is come up before me.*

Apart from that which the Septuagint translates as, "the noise of their wickedness has risen up even to me", it has translated the rest similarly. Jonah is sent to the Gentiles to condemn Israel, because Nineveh had to repent, but the Israelites still persisted in their sin. And when God says, "their wickedness has come up to me", or "the noise of their wickedness..." it is exactly the text of Genesis: "the noise of Sodom and of Gomorrah is very loud"(Gen. 18:20), and to Cain: "the blood of your brother cries to me from the earth"(Gen. 4:10). According to tropology the Lord, our Jonah, that is to say 'dove' or 'suffering', (he is given both meaning, either because the Holy Spirit descends in the form of a dove and stays with him (Mk. 1:10; Lk. 3:22; Jn. 1:32-33), or because he has suffered for our wounds, wept for Jerusalem (Lk. 19:41), and because we have been cured by his malice (Is. 53:5) is truly the son of Truth, for God is Truth (Jn. 14:6). He is sent to Nineveh the beautiful, which is to the world, where there is nothing more beautiful to our eyes than flesh. In Greek the idea of adornment is in the word *cosmos*. And when everything had been completed, each one by one, it was said, "and God saw that it was good" (Gen. 1:10). It is to Nineveh that he goes, the great city, so that although Israel has not wanted to listen, the whole world of peoples will hear God's word. And this is because their wickedness has gone up to God. For although God had made the most beautiful house for man who was devoted to serving his

111

Creator, man deprived himself of this by his own will; from childhood his heart fixed upon wickedness (Gen. 8:21; 6:5). He turned his face to the heaven (Ps. 72:9) and constructed a tower of pride (Gen 11). He deserves then God to come down to him so that he may be able to rise to heaven by the destruction of repentance, he that did not succeed by the swell of pride.

1:3a *But Jonah rose up to flee unto Tarshish from the presence of the LORD.* The Septuagint here is similar. The prophet knows by an inspiration of the Holy Spirit, that the repentance of the people is the destruction of the Jews. In this situation it is not that he is trying to save Nineveh, but that moreover he does not want to see it destroyed. Inanother place Moses prays for his people: "if you can spare them this sin, spare them; if not, erase me from your book that you have written" (Ex. 32:31-32); to this prayer, Israel was saved and Moses was not erased from the Book: even better the Lord indeed profited from his servant by sparing his other servants. For when God says, "release me", he shows that he can be held. This is similar to what the apostle says: "I wished to be anathema for my brothers who are Israelites according to their flesh" (Rom. 9:3). Not that he desires to die however, for whom to live is Christ and to die is a profit (Phil. 1:21); but he deserves life more when he wants to save others. Besides, seeing the other prophets sent to the lost flocks of the house of Israel (Mt. 10: 6) to incite the people to repent, and Balaam (Num. 23:24) the divine author of a prophecy about the deliverance of the Israelite people, Jonah feels himself punished by being chosen alone to speak against the Assyrians, the enemies of Israel, in the foreign capital where idolatry and ignorance of God still ruled. And what is more he feared that in spite of his prophesying they would still not be converted to repent, and that Israel would not be completely abandoned. For he knew by this Spirit which had entrusted him with the role of hero among the Gentiles, that once the nations had come together in belief, then Israel would surely perish. And he feared that whatever was to happen in the future would not happen in his time. Thus Jonah does as Cain does: he flees from the face of the Lord (Gen. 4:16) and

112

wants to flee to Tarshish, which Josephus interprets as that Tarsus of Cilicia[1], but changes the first letter. This can also be seen in the book of the Paralipomenon (2 Chron. 20:36-37), which says that there is a place in India which is called the same. According to the Hebrews Tarshish means more generally 'sea', according to this passage: "by a fierce wind you will break the ships of Tarshish!" (Ps. 47:8), or the ships of the sea. And in Isaiah: "cry out, O ships of Tarshish!" (Is. 23:1). I remember that I have already spoken about this several years ago in a letter to Marcella[2]. The prophet did not intend to flee to such a place, but throwing himself into the sea, he just wants to go anywhere. And this is more pertinent when talking of a fugitive or one who is afraid, that he does not choose carefully where he wants to flee to, but just jumps at the first opportunity to take to the seas. We can also say this: he thought that God was "known" only "in Judea", "and in Israel his name is great" (Ps. 75:2). After he had seen that God was also in the waves he confesses and declares: "I am a Hebrew and I fear the Lord of heaven" (Jon. 1:9), who made the seaand the dry land. But if he had made the sea and the dry earth, why believe when you leave the land that you can escape the Creator of the sea on the sea? At the same time when he sees the other sailors saved and converted, he learns that all the wickedness of Nineveh can be saved and converted by a similar confession. We can say too about our Lord and Savior that he abandoned his home and country: at the incarnation he fled in some manner the heavens for Tarshish, the sea of that age, according to what is written in another place: "here is the sea, great and wide; there are numerous beings, animals great and small; there the boats come in and go out, and this dragon that you created to be crushed" (Ps. 103:25-6). And he says too in his passion, "Father, if it is possible, let this cup pass me by!" (Mt. 26:39), lest at the unified complaints of the people, saying, "Crucify him, crucify him!" (Lk. 23:21), and "we have no king except Caesar" (Jn. 19:15), the crowd of people should enter all together; and lest the branches of the olive-tree should be broken, and in their place the shoots of the wild olive should grow (Rom. 11:17-25). He had such honor and love of his country in light of the choice of the patriarchs and of the promise of Abraham, that he said on the cross, "Father, forgive them; they know not what they do" (Lk. 23:34). Or even since Tarshish can be

113

translated as 'the contemplation of joy', the prophet, coming to Joppa, whose name means 'beautiful', hastens to hurry towards the joy and to rejoice in the pleasure of rest, to give himself completely over of contemplation. For he thinks that it is better to rejoice in beauty and in the variety of knowledge than to save the other people by letting that people die, from whom Christ would have been born.

1:3b *And went down to Joppa; and he found a ship going to Tarshish: so he paid the fare thereof, and went down into it, to go with them unto Tarshish from the presence of the LORD.*

LXX: *and he went up to Joppa, and he found a boat going to Tarshish; after paying his fare he went on board to sail with them to Tarshish, far from the face of the Lord.*

Joppa is a port of Judea (2 Chron. 2:(15)16), and it has been seen in the book of Kingdoms (i.e. 'Kings') and of the Paralipomenon. It was there that the King Hiram of Tyre transported wood from Liban by raft, then they were taken by chariot by road to Jerusalem. In this place even to this day rocks can be seen on the shore on which the chainedAndromeda was saved by Perseus[1]. The learned reader will know the story. And in light of the nature of the countryside, it is said quite rightly that the prophet came from a direction that is mountainous and precipitous, and went down to Joppa in the plain. He found there a ship that was moored and he went upon the sea. He paid his fare or the price of embarking, that is of his journey, according to the Hebrew, or the fare for himself, as the Septuagint has translated it. "and he went down into it" as the Hebrew itself says, (for *iered* in Hebrew is translated as 'went down'), for in his flight he took great care to find a hiding place. Or "he goes up", as it is written in the Vulgate edition, for going where the boat is going, thinking that he has escaped if he has left Judea. But our Lord is also at the edge of the shore of Judea, which is called 'very beautiful' because since he was in Judea, he did not want to take the bread of sons to give it to dogs. (Mt. 15:26) But because he had come for the lost flocks of the house of Israel (Mt. 10:6) he paid the price to those who transport him. Thus he who at first wants to heal his people,

1 Ovid, Metamorphoses 4.663-752; Josephus, The Jewish War 3.420

114

saves the inhabitants of the sea, and through great winds and storms, (that is his suffering and the reproof of the cross) he is plunged into Hell and saves those whom had not noticed by appearing to sleep on the boat (Mt. 8:24-25). The wise reader will not want to try to make tropology and history concur. For the Apostle refers Agar and Sara (Gal. 4:22-31) to the two Testaments, and all the same we are not able to interpret everything that is recounted in this story in a tropological way. And when explaining about Adam and Eve to the Ephesians, he says, "this is why man leaves his mother and father to join with a wife, and both will become one flesh. (Gen. 2:24) There is a great mystery: I mean Christ and the Church." (Eph. 5:31-32) Are we then first to refer the beginning of Genesis, the creation of the world, the formation of mankind, to Christ and to the Church under the pretext that the Apostle has used regarding this text? Let us admit what is written here: "thus man will leave his father" (Gen. 2:24), we can apply this to Christ by saying that he left God his Father in heaven to unite the people of the world in the Church. But how can we interpret what follows, "his mother"? Unless perhaps we are to say that he left heavenly Jerusalem, that mother of saints, and other ideas that are more complicated? And this too is written by the same Apostle: "they were drinking from a spiritual rock which was accompanying them, and this rock was Christ" (1 Cor. 10:4), but let us not try to relate the entire book of Exodus to Christ. For what can we say? That this stone was hit by Moses not just once, but twice (Ex. 17:6; Num. 20:11), that the waters flowed (Ps. 77:20) and that the floods were filled up. Are we to regard the entire story of this passage in this case as allegory? Is it not rather that each passage ought to receive a spiritual meaning according to the diversity of history? Therefore just as these texts each in this way have their interpretations and do not entail the same allegory in their context, so the prophet will not be able to be taken completely to the Lord without difficulty for the interpreter. And if it is said in the Gospel, "O wicked and adulterous generation, that she asks for a sign? As a sign she will only have the sign of the prophet Jonah. For just as Jonah spent three days and three nights in the belly of a fish, so the son of man will spend three days and three nights in the bosom of the earth" (Mt. 12:39-40). The remainder of this account does not concern Christ to the same extent. Indeed wherever this reading can be said to apply without discrepancy, we also try to make it fit.

1:4 *But the LORD sent out a great wind into the sea, and there was a mighty tempest in the sea, so that the ship was like to be broken.*

LXX: *and the Lord induced a great wind over the sea and a great storm was over the sea, and the boat threatened to break up.*

The flight of the prophet can be related to man in general, who, forsaking the commands of God, flees from his face and goes out into the world. But in consequence a storm of wickedness and the shipwreck of the entire world are sent against him, and he is made to pay attention to God and to return to that which he had fled. From this we can understand that what appears to be advantageous to mankind, turns into their downfall by God's will. And not only is their aid no use to those whom it is offered, but even those who offer it are destroyed. Therefore we read that the Assyrians conquered Egypt because she helped Israel against the will of the Lord (Is. 20:3-6). The boat is in danger because it has taken on board a dangerous passenger. The waves are aroused by the wind, a storm begins over a calm sea. When God is opposed nothing is safe.

1:5a *Then the mariners were afraid, and cried every man unto his god, and cast forth the wares that were in the ship into the sea, to lighten it of them.*

LXX: *and the sailors were afraid and each one cried out to his God and they threw the boat's cargo into the sea to lighten the boat.*

They believe that the ship with its normal cargo is too heavy, and do not understand that all the weight comes from the fleeing prophet. The sailors are afraid, each one cries out to his God. They do not know the truth, but they do not forget providence, and with a false religion they know that there is something to pray to. They cast their cargo into the sea so that the ship might cross the immensity of the waves more lightly. But for Israel, neither prosperity nor wickedness

116

can lead her back to know God. Christ weeps for the people, but He has dry eyes.

1:5b *But Jonah was gone down into the sides of the ship; and he lay, and was fast asleep.*

LXX: *Now Jonah went down to the heart of the boat and slept and snored.*

According to the history of this passage it describes the peace of the spirit of the prophet. He is troubled by the storm, or by the dangers; he just keeps the same manner of spirit when the storm is imminent, as when the weather is calm. The others though cry out to their gods, and cast the cargo overboard: each man to his own. But Jonah is so peaceful, so calm, his spirit is so at rest that he goes down to the heart of the ship to enjoy a peaceful sleep. Indeed we can also say: he knows he is a fugitive and a sinner, because he has not obeyed the commands of the Lord. It is because all the other men do not know why there is a storm that Jonah knows that he alone is the cause of it. This is why he goes down to the interior of the ship and hides himself sadly, so that he does not see the waves, like the avengers of God, rise up against him. And if he sleeps, this is not necessarily a sign of his security, but of worry. For we read that the apostles gave in to sleep on account of great sadness at the sight of the Lord's suffering (Lk. 22:45). For if we interpret the sleep of the prophet as a sign, his terrible torture, they represent a man who has fallen asleep from the drug of his wickedness: not only has he fled from God but moreover he ignores the wrath of Godas his spirit is clouded by a sort of madness. He sleeps therefore in a kind of false security and his deep sleep sounds out through his nostrils.

1:6 *So the shipmaster came to him, and said unto him, What meanest you, O sleeper? arise, call upon thy God, if so be that God will think upon us, that we perish not.*

LXX: *and the helmsman come to him and he said to him, what are you doing sleeping? Get up, and call upon your God. If he can find a way to save us then we may not die.*

It is natural that each one has more confidence in someone else when they feel themselves to be in such danger. This is why the helmsman or captain, who should have been encouraging the frightened crewmembers, but saw the seriousness of the danger, woke and reprimanded the sleeper for his thoughtless security and asked him to pray to his God immediately. He shared everyone's danger, and therefore he had to pray along with everyone else. According to tropology there are many men sailing with Jonah, who each have their own God and hasten towards the 'contemplation of joy'. But when Jonah has been discovered by chance and his death has appeased the all-encompassing storm and made calm the waters, then the one God is revered and spiritual victims are sacrificed, which according to the text were not found when they were amongst the waves.

1:7 And they said everyone to his fellow, Come, and let us cast lots, that we may know for whose cause this evil is upon us. So they cast lots, and the lot fell upon Jonah.

LXX: *and they said to each other: come, let us draw lots to see who it is that has brought this wickedness upon us. And they drew lots, and the lot fell to Jonah.*

They knew the ways of the sea and knew the causes of the storms and winds in such weather. Without a doubt they had seen the waves rise up as usual, and as they must have seen many times before, but they must never before have found the person to blame for the shipwreck, and through him tried to avoid certain danger. We should not be driven by this example to believe in fate, or to believe that this text should be connected to that of the Acts of the Apostles where Matthias is chosen by lot (Acts 1:26), because personal privileges do not make common law. For just as an old lady speaks up for the condemning of Balaam (Num. 22:28), as Pharaoh (Gen. 41) and

118

Nebuchadnezzar (Dan. 2), in their own judgment, knew the future through dreams and yet do not see that there is a divine judgment in this, like Caiaphas prophesies unknowing, that it is better for one to die for all (Jn. 11:50; 18:14): just as this fugitive is betrayed by fate, not by the powers of the fates, above all the powers of the pagan fates, but by the will of him who controlled uncertain fate. With regard to the meaning of the expression "to know by whom this wickedness had come upon us", we ought to take 'wickedness' as a synonym of affliction, of disaster, as in this passage: "every day his wickedness was enough" (Mt. 6:34), and in the prophet Amos: "is there wickedness in a town without God being the author?" (Amos 3:6). And in Isaiah: "It is I the Lord, who make goodness and wickedness" (Is. 45:7). But in other places too wickedness can be seen to be the opposite of virtue, as in the passage of our prophet that we have read above: "the cry of their wickedness went up to me" (Jon. 1:1).

1:8 *Then said they unto him, Tell us, we pray you, for whose cause this evil is upon us; What is thine occupation? and whence do you come? what is thy country? and of what people art you?*

LXX: *and they said to him, 'tell us how this wickedness has come upon us: what is your occupation, where do you come from, where you are going to, from which country, and which people you are from?*

Fate had shown him to them: they force him to admit why such a great storm, or for what reason divine wrath had come against them. Tell us, they say, where this wickedness comes from, which has come upon us, what work you do, from what land, from what people you flee, and where you are going to so quickly? Let us note the brevity here that is also seen in Virgil[1]: young men, what cause has brought you to try out unknown ways? Where are you going? He says. Your people? From which land? Do you bring war or peace? This questioning brings his identity, his country, his journey, the

1 Aeneid
8.112-114

town he comes from, so that the reason for the wickedness can be known.

1:9 And he said unto them, I am an Hebrew; and I fear the LORD, the God of heaven, which hath made the sea and the dry land.

LXX: and he replied: I am a worshipper of the Lord, and I revere God of the heavens who made the sea and the dry land

He did not say, 'I am a Jew', the name given to the people after the schism between the ten and two tribes (1 Kgs. 12:19; 14:21), but ' I am a Hebrew', that is to say *perates*[1] , passing by as Abraham who was able to say: "I am a guest and a traveler as all my fathers" (Ps. 38:13), and about whom it is written in another Psalm: "they passed from one nation to another, from one realm to another people" (Ps. 104:13). Moses says, "I will go so that I might see this great vision." (Ex. 3) I fear the Lord God of the heavens, not the gods that you have invoked and who cannot save us, but the God of heaven who made the sea and the dry land. The sea that I flee to, the earth that I flee from. And appropriately the land is not just called land, but rather dry land so that it contrasts with the sea. In short here he mentions the Creator of the universe who is the Lord of heaven, earth, and sea. But one question begs to be asked: how do they know that he speaks the truth? 'I fear the Lord God of heaven', since he has not done what this God has actually commanded him to do. The reply would surely be that the sinners themselves would fear God, and that it is appropriate for servants of the Lord not to love, but to fear. Here however you can see fear in the cult according to the meaning of those who were listening and until now knew not God.

1 Greek. 'a pilgrim and traveler

1:10 Then were the men exceedingly afraid, and said unto him, Why have you done this? For the men knew that he fled from the presence of the LORD, because he had told them.

LXX: Then the men were very afraid and said to him, "why have you done this?" for the men knew that he had fled from the face of the Lord, since he had told them.

120

The chronological order is reversed here, for you could have said there was no reason to fear because of his declaration: "I am a Hebrew and I fear the Lord God of heaven, who made the sea and the dry land". Immediately we are told why they were afraid: because he had told them that he was fleeing the presence of the Lord without having carried out his commands. Then they make excuses and say, "why did you do this?", and this means, "if you fear God, why did you do this? If this God that you revere is so powerful according to you, then how can you believe that you will be able to escape him?" They are seized by a great fear, for they realize that he is holy, and from a holy nation (having set out from Joppa they must have known the privilege of the Hebrew people), yet nonetheless they are not able to hide the fugitive. For he who flees may be powerful, but he who seeks is all the more powerful. They do not dare to hand him over to the Lord, yet they cannot hide him. They reprehend blame, and avow their fear. They pray to Jonah to give himself up for the sin he has committed. Or indeed, when they say, "why have you done this?", they are not inciting him, but questioning, wanting to know the cause of his flight, the flight of a servant from his master, of a son from his father, of a man from his God. They ask, therefore, what is this great mystery that makes you flee from the land and seek the seas, leave your country and set out for foreign lands?

1:11 *Then said they unto him, What shall we do unto you, that the sea may be calm unto us? for the sea wrought, and was tempestuous.*

LXX: *then they said to him, what should we do with you, so that the sea is calm for us? For the sea was surging its waves more and more.*

It is because of you, you say, that the winds, the waves, the sea and swells have been unleashed. You have revealed the cause of this wickedness, now tell us how to stop it. The sea swells against us, and we know that a God is angry because we took you on board. If we have sinned by taking you in, then what can we do so that the

Lord does not become angrier? "What should we do with you?" that is to say: "shall we kill you?" but you are faithful to the Lord. Are we to protect you? But you flee from Him. All we have to do is carry out whatever you command, all you have to do is give the command that the sea be calm, for now its wildness attests the wrath of the Creator. The narrator also adds the reason for this question. The sea, he says, was continually increasing in wildness. It was swelling, in the known way; it was swelling for therevenge of its Lord; it was swelling, following the fleeing prophet. And at every moment it was becoming more and more wild, and to the delaying sailors' eyes it rose in greater waves to show that it would not put off for long the Creator's revenge.

1:12 *And he said unto them, Take me up, and cast me forth into the sea; so shall the sea be calm unto you: for I know that for my sake this great tempest is upon you.*

LXX: *and he said to them, take me and throw me into the sea, and the sea will become calm for you. For I know well that it is on account of me that these great waves are against you.*

It is against me that the thunder sounds, it seeks me, it threatens to shipwreck you in order to reach me. It will seize me so that my death might let you live. For I know this, he says. This great storm is on my account. And I am not unaware that this is my punishment, this confusion of the elements, this trouble of the world. This wrath is for me, but you are going to be the victims of a shipwreck. The waves themselves command you to throw me into the sea. And since I will have felt the full effect of the storm you will be in calm seas again. We must note here the greatness of spirit of our fugitive: he is not evasive, he does not hide or deny his guilt, but having confessed his flight he accepts his punishment willingly. He would rather die so that the other sailors do not perish on account of him, and so that he does not add murder to desertion. That's it for the story. But we are also not unaware of the wild winds, which the Lord orders in the Gospel to quiet, that the ship in danger in which Jonah was sleeping, and that the raised sea which is reprimanded: "silence, and calm

122

down" (Mk. 4:39), refer to the Lord the Savior and to the Church in peril, or even to Christ awaking the apostles, and they themselves leaving their sufferings behind throw him somehow headlong into the waves. Our Jonah says, "for I know that it is on account of me that this great storm is upon you", for the winds are watching me journey to Tarshish with you, that is travel to the contemplation of joy to lead you with me to goodness so that wherever I am, so is the Father and you will be there too (Jn. 14:3; 17:27). This is why this anger rumbles, why the world which is in wickedness (1 Jn. 5:19) groans. It is in this way that the elements are disturbed. Death wants to devour me so that you may be killed as well: she does not see that as she took food in a net, my death will cause her death. Take me and throw me into the sea. For we do not have to run away from death, but receive it with open arms when it takes us from others. Thus, in the persecutions it is not allowed to kill oneself, unless chastity is in danger, but one must put ones neck to the executioner. Go, he says, calm the winds, pour libations on the sea: the storm which savages against you on account of me will be calmed by my death.

1:13 *Nevertheless the men rowed hard to bring it to the land; but they could not: for the sea wrought, and was tempestuous against them.*

LXX: *and the sailors strive to turn the ship to dry land but they cannot, for the sea swelled up against them.*

The prophet has pronounced sentence against himself; but the sailors do not dare touch him because they have learned that he is a follower of God. They were striving to return to the dry land, to get out of this danger; they refused to shed blood, preferring rather to die than kill. O how changed are they now! The people that had served God (Deut. 10:12) saying, "crucify him, crucify him" (Lk. 23:21). They are ordered to kill him: the sea is raging, the storm commands this, and they forget their own danger and only think to save another. Therefore the phrase of the Septuagint is appropriate: *parebiazonto*, they wanted to use all their force and conquer nature

123

so as not to offend the prophet of God. If the sailors rowed to regain the land, it was because they believed they could deliver the ship from danger without realizing what Jonah, who ought to have suffered, had said. All the while Jonah was in the sea the ship sat safely in the water.

1:14 *Wherefore they cried unto the LORD, and said, We beseech you, O LORD, we beseech you, let us not perish for this man's life, and lay not upon us innocent blood: for you, O LORD, have done as it pleased you.*

LXX: *and they cried to the Lord and said, but no, Lord, let us not die to let this man live. Lay not innocent blood upon us. For O Lord you have done as you wished.*

The sailors' faith is strong: they are all in danger of losing their lives, and yet pray for the lives of another. They know well that spiritual death is worse than natural death of the body. Do not lay innocent blood upon us, they say. They take the Lord as witness not to visit them for what they are about to do, and say something like this: 'we do not want to kill your prophet, but he himself has proclaimed your wrath, and the storm shows us that you have done what you wished, O Lord. Your wish is accomplished by our doing'. This seems to be the confession of Pilate, as he washes his hands and says, "I am clean of the blood of this man" (Mt. 27:24). The gentiles do not want Christ to die, and affirm that it is innocent blood. And the Jew say, "let his blood fall upon us again and on our son" (Mt. 27:25). This is why when they raise their hands to the sky, they will not be heard, for they are full of blood. For your will has been done, Lord. We welcomed the passenger, and the whirlwind began, the winds blew and the sea swelled in waves. The fugitive was brought by fate, and tells what we must do: all of this, Lord, is the effect of your will. Yes, Lord, your will has been done. In this way the Savior speaks in the Psalm, "Lord, I wanted to do your will" (Ps. 39:9).

1:15 *So they took up Jonah, and cast him forth into the sea: and the sea ceased from her raging.*

LXX: *and they took Jonah and they threw him into the sea, and the sea became ceased from its agitation.*

He did not say, they grabbed him and threw him but they raised him up as if they were carrying him with respect and honor, and they threw him into the sea without him struggling, but rather he went willingly. And the sea ceased because it had found the man it was searching for. Just as when you pursue a fugitive, and running, catch up with him, then stop to grab hold of him; so too the sea was wild without Jonah, and then when it had in its lap what it desired it rejoiced in having him and cherished him, and the calm returned by this joy. If we consider before the suffering of Christ, the confessions of the world, the contrary winds of different opinions, the ship and all human kind, that is all creation to be in danger, then, after the suffering of Christ there is the calm of faith, the peace of the world, universal safety, conversion to God, and we will see how after Jonah has been thrown overboard the sea ceases from its raging.

1:16 *Then the men feared the LORD exceedingly, and offered a sacrifice unto the LORD, and made vows.*

LXX: similar.

Before the anger of the Lord the sailors implored their gods under the effect of their fear; after his anger they fear the Lord, that is they revere and worship Him. They do not worship Him in the usual way, as we have seen in the beginning, but with "a great fear", according to that which is said: "from all their spirit and all their heart and all their soul" (Deut. 6:5; Mt. 22:37). And they sacrificed victims that indeed, to take this literally, they were not able to have out at sea. But this is because sacrifice to God is a troubled spirit. (Ps. 50:19) And it is said in another place: "offer to God a sacrifice of praise, acquit your vows to the Highest." (Ps. 49:14) And again: "we acquit ourselves to you of our vows that we have promised". (Hos. 14:3) This is how they offer a sacrifice in the middle of the sea, and they promise others vowing never to be far from Him whom they have

125

begun to revere and worship. They were seized by a great fear for they recognized from the calm sea and the disappearing storm that the prophet had spoken true. Jonah at sea, a fugitive and shipwrecked, once dead saves the ship in the waves, saves the pagans who had been beforehand divided in different beliefs by the wickedness of the world. And Hosea, Amos, Isaiah, and Joel, who prophesied at the same time did not manage to convert the people in Judea. This shows that the shipwreck could only be saved by the death of the fugitive.

Chapter 2

2:1a *Now the LORD had prepared a great fish to swallow up Jonah.*

LXX: *and the Lord ordered a great fish to swallow Jonah.*

The Lord commanded death and the underworld to receive the prophet. To the eager jaws of death he seemed a prey: she had such joy in swallowing him, and such sadness in spitting him out. Thus happened what is written in Hosea: "I will be your death, O Death! I will be your bite, Hell!" (Hos. 13:14). In the Hebrew we read "a great fish", which the Septuagint and the Lord in the Gospel call a whale, to explain the matter in short. For the Hebrew says *dag gadol* that we translate as 'a big fish'. Evidently this means a whale. We must note too that where he awaited death, he found his salvation. And when it says, "he had prepared", this is even right at the beginning of creation, the animal which is mentioned in the psalm: "this dragon which you have created to play with him" (Ps. 103:26). Or even he makes a fish come near to the ship to take in its belly Jonah who has been thrown overboard, and to provide his rescue not his death. So he who felt the wrath of God in the boat was to feel his benevolence in his death.

2:1b *And Jonah was in the belly of the fish three days and three nights.*

LXX: *and Jonah was in the belly of the whale for three days and three nights.*

The Lord shows in the Gospel the symbolism of this passage (Mt. 12:40), and it is superfluous to say in the same terms or even in other terms what he who has suffered has already said. But we ask ourselves this: how was he three days and three nights in the belly of the earth. Some scholars take the view according to *paraskeuen*, because of the solar eclipse from the sixth to the ninth hour when night followed day, this would be two days and nights, and adding the Sabbath, believe that we should count this as three days and three nights. But I prefer to understand this by reason of synecdoche, seeing the whole as a part: where he is dead in *paraskeuen* (Lk. 23:54), let us count one day and one night; two with the Sabbath; the third night which arises from the day of the Lord, let us take that as the beginning of the next day, for, in Genesis (Gen. 1:5, 8) the night is not of the preceding day, but of the following day, that is to say the beginning of the next day, not the end of the previous. To understand this better I will say it more simply: if a man leaves his house at nine and the next day he arrives at his other house at three. And if I say that he has been two days in travelling, I will not be reprimanded as a liar, because he has not used all the hours of two days, but only a part for his journey. Nonetheless this seems to me to be the interpretation. If someone does not agree with this, and he can explain the meaning in a clearer way, then we should follow his interpretation.

2:2 *Then Jonah prayed unto the LORD his God out of the fish's belly.*

LXX: similar.

If Jonah is compared to the Lord, and his time of three days and three nights in the belly of the whale is a sign of the suffering of the Savior, his prayer also ought to be a kind of prayer of the Savior. Some people, I don't doubt, will find it difficult to believe that a man can spend three days and three nights in the belly of a whale, especially after a shipwreck. These people can either be religious or not. But if they have faith, they will believe this all the more: how three children thrown into a furnace of hot fire were so well protected that their clothes were not even singed (Dan. 3:94/27); how the sea drew back on itself into two sides and held itself up like a wall to offer a route for the people who wanted to pass (Ex. 14:22, 29); how with all human moderation the anger of a lion that had been increased by hunger was taken by fear at the sight of his prey, and didn't want to touch it (Dan. 6:23); and even other such miracles. If they do not have faith, let them read the fifteen books of Ovid's Metamorphoses, and all Greek and Latin history. Therein they will see Daphne changed into a bay-tree, or the sister of Phaeton changed into poplars; how Jupiter the highest god, was transformed into a swan, flowed in gold and became a raging bull, and other adventures where the ugliness of the stories attest the holiness of the divinity. They believe in these stories and say that everything is possible for one god. And while they believe these ugly stories and defend the absolute power of a god, they do not attribute this same power to honest deeds. With regard to these words: 'then Jonah prayed to the Lord his God out of the belly of the fish and said...' we understand that feeling that he is safe in the belly of the whale he does not despair of divine mercy and concentrates wholly on praying. For God, who had said, "I am with him in his distress" (Ps. 90:15), and when he calls to me, I will reply, "I am here." (Is. 58:9), came to his aid and he whose prayer had been answered was then able to say, "in distress you have made me greater" (Ps. 4:2).

2:3 *And said, I cried by reason of mine affliction unto the LORD, and he heard me; out of the belly of hell cried I, and you heard my voice.*

LXX: similar except: *'from the belly of hell I threw out my cries'*.

He does not say, "I cry", but "I cried". He does not pray for the future, but gives thanks for the past. That shows us that from the moment he is thrown into the sea and sees the whale, that great bulk, that immense mouth which opened wide to swallow him, he remembered God and cried out, either by the waves giving passage for his cry, or by a feeling from the depths of his heart, according to that which the apostle says: "crying in your hearts" (Col. 3:16): "Abba! Father" (Rom. 8:15). He cried to him who alone knew the hearts of men and said to Moses, "why do you cry out to me?" (Ex. 14:15), while the Scriptures remember that Moses had never cried out before this speech. This is the text that we read in the first psalm of the steps: "I cried to the Lord in my distress and he replied to me." (Ps. 119:1) By the "belly of hell" we understand the stomach of a whale of such great size that it took the place of hell. But this can better be referred to the person of Christ, who under the name of David, sings in the psalm: "you will not leave my spirit in hell, and you will not allow your saint to see putrefaction" (Ps. 15:10), living in hell free among the dead.

129

2:4a *For you had cast me into the deep, in the midst of the seas; and the floods compassed me about.*

LXX: *you cast me into the deep of the heart from the sea, and the waves surrounded me.*

The interpretation of the person of Jonah is not difficult: from the moment when he was closed in the stomach of the whale and foundhimself at the deepest and middle of the sea, he was surrounded by waves. For the Lord, the Savior, prefiguring Psalm 68 in which he says, "I am enshrouded in the deep mud where there is no ground. I have come to the deepest part of the sea and the storm engulfs me" (Ps. 68:3). It is said of him in another psalm: "but you, you have rejected, despised and disquieted your Christ; you have cursed the covenant of your master, you have dishonored his sacred place on earth, you have destroyed all its walls" (Ps. 88:39-41), and so on. For in this comparison of divine blessing and that place about which is written, "his home is in sacred peace" (Ps. 75:3), all habitation on earth is full of waves, full of storms. And the "heart of the sea" means hell, for which we read in the Gospel, "in the heart of the earth" (Mt. 12:40). For just as the heart is at the middle of animal, so we say that hell is in the middle of the earth. Or according to anagoge he recalls that he is "in the heart of the sea", that is in the middle of temptations. However, although he has been among the bitter waters and been tempted by all things without sin, he has not felt the bitter waters, but has been surrounded by the waves about which we read elsewhere, "an impetuous wave rejoices in the city of God" (Ps. 45:5). Others drank the salty waves; myself, surrounded by temptation, I endured sweeter currents. And do not think what the Lord says now is impious: "you have cast me into the deep", who says in the psalm, "for they have followed him that you smote" (Ps. 68:27), according to the phrase which in Zechariah is spoken by the Father: "I will smite the shepherd, and the flocks will be scattered" (Zec.13:7).

2:4b *All thy billows and thy waves passed over me.*

LXX: *all your whirlwinds and your waves passed over me.*

No one can doubt that the swelling waves of the sea encompassed Jonah, that there was fierce thunder in the storm. But we ask how all the whirlwinds, billows and the waves of God encompassed the Savior. "The life of men on earth is temptation" (Job. 7:1), or as there is in the Hebrew, "a military service", for we serve here to be crowned elsewhere. There is no man who can sustain all the temptations, except him who has been tempted by all, in our image, except sin (Heb. 4:15). This is why it is said in Corinthians, "no temptation will take you, I hope, unless it is human. God is faithful, he will not let you try beyond your ability, but he will produce an exit that you may hold on to." (1 Cor. 10:13) And like all persecutions and all wicked things that happen to usthey do not happen without the will of God, we speak of whirlwinds and waves of God, which have not crushed Jesus, but have come down upon him with a simple threat of shipwreck which does not happen. Thus all persecutions and whirlwinds which tortured mankind and broke all the ships have passed thundering on my head. And myself, I have sustained storms and broken whirlwinds which were raging, to allow others to sail more easily.

2:5 *Then I said, I am cast out of thy sight;*

LXX: *I said, I am cast far from your sight.*

Before I cried out from the depths of my distress and before you heard me, me who had taken the position of slave and imitated its weakness, I said, "I am cast out of your sight". When I was with you enjoying your light and you, light, being light, I did not say "I am cast out". But once at the bottom of the sea and surrounded by the flesh of a man, I say: "I am cast out of your sight". I said this as a man. And as God being in that condition I did not think of my equality with you, because I wanted to raise mankind to you, so that wherever I am with you they are there as well and those who have believed in me and in you, I say: yet I will look again toward thy holy temple. LXX: 'do you not think I will be able to see your holy temple again?'. To express the Greek *ara*, the Vulgate edition's 'do you think' can be interpreted as 'therefore', like the last conclusion of the proposition, of the assumption and of the confirmation and syllogism, not in the uncertainty of someone who

131

hesitates but in the confidence of someone who affirms. This has been translated by, "yet I will look again on your holy temple", according to that which is said in another psalm by the spokesperson of Christ: "Lord, I have loved beauty of your house and the tabernacle where your glory lives" (Ps. 25:8), and the passage of the Gospel in which it says, "Father, glorify me with you by that glory which I had before the world existed" (Jn. 17:5). And the Father replied to heaven: "I have glorified him, and I shall glorify him" (Jn. 12:28). Or even because he says, "the Father is in me, and I am in Him" (Jn. 10:38; 14:10-11; 17:21), for the temple of the Father is the Son, thus the temple of the Son is the Father. He Himself said, "I left my Father and have come" (Jn. 16:28), and "the word was with God and the word was God" (Jn. 1:1). Or even the Savior, the one and the same, asks as man and promises as God, and he is sure of the right that was always his. For the person of Jonah you can clearly seethat with a feeling of desire and confidence, at the bottom of the sea, he wished to see the temple of the Lord, and with a prophetic spirit he found himself elsewhere and thought of other things.

2:6a *The waters compassed me about, even to the soul: the depth closed me round about,*

LXX: *the water ran about me up to my spirit; the last depth closed around me.*

These waters, near to the deep, which cycle and slide about the earth, which drag much mud with them, tend to kill not the body but the soul, for they are friendly to the body and warmed by its desires. This is why, according to that which I have said above, the Lord says in the psalm, "save me, Lord, because the waters have penetrated even to my soul" (Ps. 68:2), and in another passage, "my soul has passed a torrent" (Ps. 123:5), and, "let not the well press its mouth on me" (Ps. 68:16), let hell not imprison me! Let it not refuse me an exit! I freely made the descent; so let me make the ascent back again freely. I became a captive voluntarily, I ought to free the captives so that this verse is fulfilled: "ascending into the higher parts he led the captives" (Eph. 4:8). For those who were beforehand captives in death, he brought them to life again. We must heed certain wicked forces in the deep, or the specific powers in torture and supplication; demons, in the Gospel, ask not to be forced to go to them (Mt. 8:30; Mk. 5:10; Lk. 8:31). This is why "the darkness was over the deep" (Gen. 1:2). Sometimes the deep is taken to mean the sacraments in a deeper sense, the judgments of God: "the judgments of the Lord are a great abyss" (Ps. 35:7), and "the deep cries out to the deep in a cry of your cataracts." (Ps. 41:8)

2:6b-7a *the weeds were wrapped about my head. I went down to the bottoms of the mountains; the earth with her bars was about me forever:*

LXX: *my head has penetrated to the base of mountains; I descended to into the earth whose bars are eternal bonds.*

No one doubts that the ocean covered Jonah's head, that he went down to the roots of mountains and came to the depths of the earth by which as bars and columns by the will of God the earthly sphere is supported. This earth about which is said elsewhere, "I consolidated her columns" (Ps. 74:4). With regard to the Lord Savior, according to the two editions, this seems to me to be what is meant. His heart and his head, that is the spirit that he thought worthy to take with a body for our safety, went down to the base of the mountains which were covered by waves; they were restrained by the will of God, the deep covered them, they were parted by the majesty of God. His spirit then went down into hell, into those places to which in the last of the mud, the spirits of sinners were held, so too the psalmist says: "they will go down to the depths of the earth, they will be the lot of wolves" (Ps. 62:10-11). These are the bars of the earth and like the locks of a final prison and tortures, which do not let the captive spirits out of hell. This is why the Septuagint has translated this is a pertinent way: "eternal bonds", that is, wanting to keep in all those whom it had once captured. But our Lord, about which we read these lines of Cyrus in Isaiah: "I will break the bronze bars, I will crack the iron bars" (Is. 45:2), He went down to the roots of the mountains, and was enclosed by eternal bars to free all the prisoners.

133

2:7b *yet have you brought up my life from corruption, O LORD my God.*

LXX: *and from corruption my life comes up to me, O Lord my God.*

He says rightly "you have brought up" or "let my life come up from corruption", because it had descended to corruption in hell. This is what the apostles interpret in the fifteenth psalm as prophetic speech of the Lord: "for you will not leave my spirit in hell, and you will not permit your holiness to see the corruption" (Ps. 15:10), given that David is dead and has been buried, but the Savior's flesh has not known corruption. Others understand that compared to celestial blessing and to the Word of God the body of man is corruption itself, for "it is sown in corruption" (1 Cor. 15:42), and in the psalm one hundred and two, the meaning is applied to a righteous man: "he who cures all illnesses, who has brought his life back from death" (Ps. 102:3-4). This is why the Apostle says, "O wicked man that I am! Who will deliver me from this body of death?" (Rom. 7:24). It is called "the body of death", or "body of misery". These people take the text in the sense of their heresy, to see an Antichrist in the place of Christ, and to take the Churches in order to feed a fat stomach and discuss contrary to the flesh living in the flesh. But we, we know that the body taken from the pure Virgin was not the corruption of Christ, but his temple. If we pass then to the thought of the Apostle in Corinthians, where there is the question of a spiritual body, we would say, in removing any appearance of chicanery, that the same body, the same flesh rises again, which has been buried and placed in the soil; but the only thing that changes is the glory, not nature. "for this corruptible being must cover incorruptibility, this mortal being must clothe immortality." (1 Cor. 15:53) When he says "this being" it is almost as if one showed the body by pinching it between two fingers: in which we are born, in which we die, that those who are guilty fear to receive as punishment, that virginity awaits in recompense, that the adulterer fears in punishment. For Jonah, this is how we can understand it: he who would have had to corrupt himself physiologically in the belly of the whale, and get by on the food of beasts and survive by drinking from the veins and arteries, still managed to remain safe and sound. And when he says, "Lord my God", this is a feeling of flattery: he thinks that God, who is common to all, is also common to him, and feels he is his own because of the greatness of his benevolence.

2:8 *When my soul fainted within me I remembered the LORD.*

LXX: *when my spirit failed in me, I remembered the Lord.*

Although I hoped for no aid, he says, the memory of the Lord saved me, according to this passage: "I remembered the Lord and I rejoiced" (Ps. 76:4), and in another passage, "I remembered former days and I remembered the days of eternity" (Ps. 76:6). I had lost all hope of finding a way out: my body was so frail in the intestines of the whale that I could not hope for my life. And so, everything that seemed impossible I found to be surpassed by the thought of the Lord. I saw myself imprisoned in the intestines of the whale, and all my hope was the Lord. From this we can learn that, according to the Septuagint, at the time when our spirit fails us, it is wrenched from its union with the body, and we ought not to turn our thoughts from Him who inside and outside our body is the Lord. For the Savior the interpretation is not very difficult because he said, "my spirit is sad to die" (Mt. 26:38; Mk. 14:34), and "My Father, if it is possible let this cup pass me by" (Mt. 26:39), and, "I place my spirit in your hands" (Ps. 30:6; Lk. 23:46), and other passages which are similar to this. And my prayer came in unto you, into thine holy temple. LXX: similar. In my distress I remembered the Lord so and my prayer came in to heaven from the depths of the sea and from the roots of the mountains, and came to your holy temple where you reside in eternal beatitude. This new kind of speech should be noted here: a prayer made for a prayer. Jonah asks that his prayer rise up to the temple of God. He wishes like the Pope that in his body the people should be freed.

2:9 *They that observe lying vanities forsake their own mercy.*

LXX: *those that keep mistaken vanities lose their mercy.*

135

By nature God is merciful and ready by his mildness to save those whom he can't save by justice. But because of our vices we lose the mercy which is reserved for us and is offered to us. Jonah did not say, "those who make vanities", for "vanity of vanities, all is vanity" (Eccl. 1:1), not to have an air of condemning everyone, and of refusing mercy to all mankind, but "those who keep vanities" or the lie "those who have come to love their heart" (Ps. 72:7), who are not happy with doing, but who keep their vanities as if they cherished them, thinking they have found some kind of treasure. Note too the greatness of the prophet's spirit: at the bottom of the sea, surrounded by an eternal night in the intestines of a great beast he is not thoughtful of his danger, but philosophies on the question of nature. "they will lose" he says "their mercy". Although mercy is offended and we can understand that it is God Himself: for "God is merciful and good, patient and full of pity" (Ps. 144:8), yet mercy does not abandon those who keep their vanities, she does not curse them, but waits for them to return, while they intentionally abandon the mercy which is before them, offered to them. This can also be prophesied for the Lord on the subject of the infidelity of the Jews, who think themselves to observe the precepts of mankind (Mk. 7:7) and the commandments of the Pharisees, this is vanity and a lie, and they have abandoned God who always had pity for them.

2:10 *But I will sacrifice unto you with the voice of thanksgiving; I will pay that that I have vowed. Salvation is of the LORD.*

LXX: *but I will sacrifice to you with the voice of praise and the action of thanksgiving. I will pay all that I have vowed to you, Lord, in salutation.*

Those who keep their vanities have abandoned their mercy. But I who have been eaten for the sake of the safety of the multitude, will offer you sacrifices with the voice of praise and thanksgiving, offering myself. For "Christ, our Easter, has been sacrificed" (1 Cor. 5:7). A as a true Pope and lamb he offers himself for us. And I will give thanks to you, saying, "I bless you Father, lord of heaven and earth" (Mt. 11:25), and I will keep those vows to the Lord that I made for the safety of others, so that all that "you have given me never dies" (Jn. 6:39;10:28;

17:12). We see what the Lord promised in his suffering for our safety: let us not make Jesus a liar (1 Jn. 1:10), and let us be pure, delivered from all the uncleanness of sins so that he offers us to God the Father as the victims he had promised.

2:11 *And the LORD spoke unto the fish, and it vomited out Jonah upon the dry land.*

LXX: *and he ordered the whale to vomit Jonah out onto the dry land.*

That which we read above as being about Jonah, the Lord prayed for in the stomach of the whale about which Job speaks in an unclear way: "let he who curses this day curse him, he who will capture the great whale" (Job. 3:8. LXX). The great whale, the deep and hell are then ordered to give back the Lord to the dry earth; thus he who had died to free those detained by the chains of death, can lead with him many others towards life. With regard to the expression 'vomited' we must take this to be said in a very emphatic way, to mean that triumphant life has emerged from the deepest and most impenetrable parts of death.

Chapter 3

3:1-2 *And the word of the LORD came unto Jonah the second time, saying, arise, go unto Nineveh, that great city, and preach unto it the preaching that I bid you.*

LXX: *and the message of God came to Jonah a second time, saying, arise, go to Nineveh, the great city, and preach there this message that I have told you.*

He did not say to the prophet, "why have you not done what you were ordered to do?" But the punishment of the shipwreck and his drowning are enough for him to understand the Lord, the liberator, whom he hadn't known to be ordering. Moreover it is superfluous to see his wounds as those of a false servant of God, once he has been smitten, for such a punishment is less of a correction than a reproof. And our Lord is sent to Nineveh a second time after his resurrection: he who had fled by whatever means beforehand when he said, "My Father, if it is possible let this cup pass me by" (Mt. 26:39), and who had not wanted to give bread of children to dogs, now the children have cried out, "crucify him, crucify him! we have no king except Caesar" (Lk. 23:21; Jn. 19:15), he makes his way towards Nineveh of his own accord to preach after his resurrection that he underwent as he was ordered to do before his suffering. The command is given, he hears it, he refuses, then he is forced to want, and the second time he carries out the will of the Father: all of this is connected to man and to the "form of a slave" (Phil. 2:7), to whom such expressions are appropriate.

3:3 *So Jonah arose, and went unto Nineveh, according to the word of the LORD. Now Nineveh was an exceeding great city of three days' journey. [And Jonah began to enter into the city a day's journey]*

LXX: *so Jonah arose and went to Nineveh, according to the word of the Lord. Now Nineveh was a city of godly size, around three days in journey. Jonah began to enter the city, about one day's travel.*

Jonah immediately carries out the command that he has been given. Nineveh to which the prophet was journeying, was a great city, which it took around three days' journey to circle. But he remembers the command he has been given and the recent shipwreck and makes the normal journey of three days in one day. However, there are some people who believe that he simply proclaimed his message in a third of the city, and that his speech quickly was made known to the other inhabitants. And our Lord is said to arise and speak of his own accord after being in hell, and announces the word of the Lord when he sends the apostles to baptize those who were in Nineveh in the name of the Father the Son and the Holy Spirit (Mt. 28:19). So there are the three days of journey! And this sacrament of mankind's safety is "a journey of one day", that is it is finished by the proclamation of one sole God. Jonah preaches not so much to the apostles but more by the method of the apostles. He himself says, "and I will be with you always until the end of the world" (Mt. 28:20). There is no doubt that Nineveh was a city of godly magnitude because the world and all things have existed through God and because without Him nothing would ever have existed. (Jn. 1:3) Note too that he has not said, "of three days and three nights" or "of one day and one night", but simply "and of three days", and "of one day", to show that in the sacrament of the Trinity and of the confession of one sole God there is no darkness.

3:4 *[And Jonah began to enter into the city a day's journey], and he cried, and said, Yet forty days, and Nineveh shall be overthrown.*

LXX: *he proclaimed and said, another three days and Nineveh will be destroyed.*

The umber three written in the Septuagint does not agree with the penitence, and I am quite astonished at this translation, for in Hebrew neither the letters or syllables or accents or the word show any common element. For three is said, *salos* and forty *arbaim*. Moreover the prophet who was sent from Judea to the Assyrians was to claim after such a journey penitence worthy of his prediction to cure with a long-present dressing his old and putrid wounds. Moreover the number forty is appropriate to sinners, to hunger, to prayer, to sackcloth, to tears and

139

to perseverance in prayer. In this way Moses fasted for forty days on mount Sinai (Ex. 34:28; Deut. 9:18) and Elijah fleeing Jezebel (1 Kgs. 19:8) is presented to us as having fasted for forty days after having told Israel about the famine (1 Kgs. 17:1), when the anger of God was upon them. And the Lord Himself, the true Jonah who is sent to preach to the world fasts for forty days (Mt. 4:2). And he leaves us as hereditary fasting to prepare our spirits, by this number of forty, as the food of his body. "he cried out": the Gospel shows this expression more fully: "standing, he cried out in the temple: if anyone is thirsty, let him come to me and he shall drink" (Jn. 7:37), for all speech of the Savior is called a cry because he speaks about weighty subjects.

3:5 *So the people of Nineveh believed God, and proclaimed a fast, and put on sackcloth, from the greatest of them even to the least of them.*

LXX: similar.

Nineveh believed but Israel did not believe; the foreskin believed, but circumcision remained without faith. First of all the men of Nineveh believed who had arrived at the age of Christ (Eph. 4:13): they announced a fast and dressed in sackcloth, from the greatest to the smallest of them. This regime and clothing is very worthy of penitence, so that those who had offended God through their indulgence or lust appeased him by condemning all that they had previously offended with. Sackcloth and fasting are the weapons of penitence, the rescue of sinners. First of all fasting, then sackcloth; first of all what is not seen, then what is visible; the one is always shown to God, the other sometimes to man. And if it were necessary to remove one from the two then I would rather keep fasting without sackcloth than have sackcloth without fasting. Elder men give the example which pertains to youths: for no one is without sin; and if his life only lasted one day, the years of his life would still be counted (Job. 14:5. LXX). For if the stars are not pure before God, they are still more so than a worm or putrefaction, and those who are held by the sin of Adam, the great offender. Note here too the order, which is well written: God commands the prophet, the prophet proclaims to the city. First of all the men believe, announce fasting, and then everyone puts on sackcloth.

140

The men do not announce the putting on of sackcloth, but only the fasting. All the same, with reason, those to whom penitence has been proscribed wear sackcloth and fast so that empty stomach and mourning clothes give the Lord more of an opportunity to remit.

3:6-9 *For word came unto the king of Nineveh, and he arose from his throne, and he laid his robe from him, and covered him with sackcloth, and sat in ashes. 7 And he caused it to be proclaimed and published through Nineveh by the decree of the king and his nobles, saying, Let neither man nor beast, herd nor flock, taste any thing: let them not feed, nor drink water: 8 But let man and beast be covered with sackcloth, and cry mightily unto God: yea, let them turn everyone from his evil way, and from the violence that is in their hands. 9 Who can tell if God will turn and repent, and turn away from his fierce anger, that we perish not?*

LXX: *the message reached the king of Nineveh, and he arose from his throne, took off his robe and covered himself with sackcloth, and he sat down upon the earth. And by the order of the king and his nobles it was announced throughout Nineveh, saying, it is forbidden for any man or beast or oxen or sheep to eat anything, to drink any water. Men and beasts were covered in sackcloth and cried out to the Lord mightily. Let each one turn away from his wicked practices and from the unfairness that was in his hands, saying, who knows if God will turn and repent, if he will not abandon the fierceness of his wrath so that we might not die?.*

I know certain men for whom the king of Nineveh, (who is the last to hear the proclamation and who descends from his throne, and forgoes the ornaments of his former vices and dressed in sackcloth sits on the ground, he is not content with his own conversion, preaches penitence to others with his leaders, saying, "let the men and beasts, big and small of size, be tortured by hunger, let them put on sackcloth, condemn their former sins and betake themselves without reservation to penitence!) is the symbol of the devil, who at the end of the world, (because no spiritual creature that is made reasoning by God will perish), will descend from his pride and do penitence and will be restored to his

141

former position. To support this opinion they use this example of Daniel in which Nebuchadnezzar after seven years of penitence is returned to his former reign. (Dan. 4:24, 29, 33) But because this idea is not in the Holy Scripture and since it completely destroys the fear of God, (for men will slide easily into vices if they believe that even the devil, the creator of wickedness and the source of all sins, can be saved if he does penitence), we must eradicate this from our spirits. Let us remember though that the sinners in the Gospel are sent to the eternal fire (Mt. 25:41), which is prepared for the devil and his angels, about whom is said, "their worm will not die and their fire will not be extinguished" (Is. 66:24). All the same we know that God is mild, and we sinners do not enjoy his cruelty, but we read, "the Lord is kindly and righteous, and our God will be merciful" (Ps. 114:5). The justice of God is surrounded by mercy, and it is by this route that he proceeds to judgment: he spares to judge, he judges to be merciful. "Mercy and Truth are to be found in our path; Justice and Peace are to be embraced" (Ps. 84:11). Moreover if all spiritual creatures are equal and if they raise themselves up by their virtues to heaven, or by their vices take themselves to the depths, then after a long circuit and infinite centuries, if all are returned to their original state with the same worthiness to all conflicting, what difference will there be between the virgin and the prostitute? What distinction will there be between the mother of the Lord and (it is wicked to say) the victims of public pleasures? Will Gabriel be like the devil? Will the apostles be as demons? Will the prophets be as pseudo-prophets? Martyrs as their persecutors? Imagine all that you will, increase by two-fold the years and the time, take infinite time for torture: if the end for all is the same, all the past is then nothing, for what is of importance to us is not what we are at any given moment, but what we will be forever more. I am not forgetting what is often said to argue against this point, preparing hope for oneself and some kind of safety with the devil. But this is not the appropriate time to write at length against the opinion of the wicked and against the *synphragma* of the devil from those who teach one thing in private only to deny it in public. It is enough for me to have shown what I believe this passage signifies, and as is appropriate in a commentary, to remark briefly who the king of Nineveh is, he who is the last to hear the word of God. Just how much eloquence and secular knowledge are worth to mankind can be seen in Demosthenes, Cicero,

142

Plato, Xenophon, Theophrastus, Aristotle and the other philosophers and orators who are considered kings and their precepts are not taken as the work of mortals but as oracles of the gods. About which Plato says, happy are those states where philosophers rule, or if kings are philosophers. How difficult it is for such men to believe in God! I am neglecting though those examples from daily life, and pass over the stories of pagans and content myself with the text of the apostle who writes in Corinthians, saying, "look, brothers, to your vocation, among you. For there are not many who are wise about their flesh, nor many powerful, or noble. But there is much madness in the world, and this is what God has chosen to confuse wise men. That which is weak in the world, this is what God has chosen to confuse strength, and that which is in the world without good birth this is what God has chosen..." (1 Cor. 1:26-28) and again he says, "I will destroy the wisdom of the wise, and I will reprove the knowledge of those who know." (Is. 29:14; 1 Cor. 1:19) And: "see that no one robs you, through philosophy, this is a vain seduction" (Col. 2:8). From this the predication of Christ is clear, the kings of the world hear last; then they put down the clamor of eloquence and the beautiful appearance of words, they abandon themselves completely to all simplicity and rusticity, and return to the ways of peasants, sitting in the dirt and destroying what they had formerly said was good before. Let us take as an example the benevolent Cyprian: who is firstly the champion of idolatry, and had such a reputation of good speaking that he taught the art of rhetoric at Carthage. He finishes by listening to the speech of Jonah, is converted to repent and gains such courage as to preach about Christ in public and lays his neck under the sword for him. For sure we know that the King of Nineveh descended from his throne, exchanged his red gown for sackcloth, his perfumes for mud, and cleanness for uncleanness- not uncleanness of meanings but of his words. In the same way in Jeremiah it is said about Babylon that "Babylon is a golden chalice which makes all the earth drunk" (Jer. 51:7). Which man has not been made drunk by secular eloquence? Whose spirit has not been shot through by the composition of words and by the brightness of his elegant speech? Those powerful, noble and rich have great difficulty in believing in God; then how much more so for the masters of speech! Their spirit is blinded by riches, wealth, abundance, they are prevented by their sins and cannot see their virtues; they judge the simplicity of the Holy

143

Scripture not on the majesty of its meanings, but out of the baseness of its words. But when they who have previously taught wickedness are converted to repent and start to teach what is good then we will see the people of Nineveh converted with a single proclamation, and the speech that we read in Isaiah will come true: "is a people thus born in one go?" (Is. 66:8. LXX) Men and animals are covered with sackcloth, crying out to the Lord, this is to be understood by the same meaning as this: that those who have reason and those who do not, the wise and the simple repent according to that phrase said elsewhere: "You will save men and the animals O Lord" (Ps. 35:7). It is possible however to interpret differently the animals covered in sackcloth, especially according to those passages in which we read, "the sun and moon will be dressed in sackcloth" (Joel. 2:10), and in another passage, "I will cover the heavens with sackcloth". (Is. 50:3) This will be the clothing of mourning, the worry and sadness that are designated metaphorically by sackcloth. And this phrase: "who knows if God will turn and pardon?" places us in uncertainty and doubt Thus men in hypothetical cleanness repent with more intent and arouse even more God's mercy.

3:10 *And God saw their works, that they turned from their evil way; and God repented of the evil, that he had said that he would do unto them; and he did it not.*

LXX: *God saw their works since they turned from their wicked ways. And God repented for their wickedness that he had said he would do to them and he did not do it.*

According to the two meanings of this passage God is threatening the town of Assyria and threatens the people of the world every day so that they repent: if they convert then he will change his judgment, and it will be changed by the conversion of the people. Jeremiah and Ezekiel explain this more clearly: the Lord has not fulfilled the good that he has promised to do if the good turn to sinners; nor the wickedness that he threatened the wicked if they return to safety. Thus now God sees their works, since they turn from their wicked way. But he did not hear those vain promises that Israel was in the custom of making: "all that God has said, we shall do" (Ex. 24:3,7), but he sees the works. And because

144

he prefers a sinner's repentance rather than his death (Ez. 33:11) he willingly changes his sentence because he has seen a change in the works. Or rather God has continued in his proposition, since he wanted to pity right from the beginning. No one in fact who desires to punish, threatens what he will actually do. The word 'wickedness' as we have noted above, can be taken to mean supplication or torture, not that God could think to do nothing on account of the wickedness.

Chapter 4

4:1 *But it displeased Jonah exceedingly and he was very angry. [And he prayed unto the LORD, and said]*

LXX: *Jonah was saddened by a great sadness, and he was confounded. And he prayed to the Lord, and he said.*

Seeing the crowd of gentiles enter (Rom. 11:25), and that fulfills what is written in Deuteronomy: "they annoyed me with these gods who are not gods, so I will annoy them with a people that is not one; I shall anger them like a foolish nation" (Deut. 32:21). He despairs of Israel's safety and is hit by a great suffering which breaks out in words. He shows the signs of his suffering and more or less says this: 'I have been the only one of the prophets chosen to announce my people's ruin to them through the safety of others.' Thus he is not sad that the crowd of gentiles should be saved, as some people believe, but it is the destruction of Israel. Moreover our Lord wept for Jerusalem and refused to take bread away from the children to give to the dogs (Mt. 15:26; Mk. 7:27). And the apostles preach firstly to Israel, and Paul wishes to be anathema for his brothers who are Israelites (Act. 13:46) and have adoption, glory, alliance, promises and law, and from whom the patriarchs come, and from them too according to the flesh came Christ. (Rom. 9:3-5) But suffering in vain, which is interpreted as the word Jonah, he is smitten by suffering, and 'the spirit is sad until death' (Mt. 26:38; Mk. 14:34). For lest the people of the Jews should die, he has suffered as much as he was in power. The name of the sufferer also is appropriate to the story, since it signifies the toil of the prophet, weighed down by the miseries of his journey and the shipwreck.

4:2-3 *[And he prayed unto the LORD, and said], I pray you, O LORD, was not this my saying, when I was yet in my country? Therefore I fled before unto Tarshish: for I knew that you are a gracious God, and merciful, slow to anger, and of great kindness, and you repent of the evil. Therefore now, O LORD, take, I beseech you, my life from me; for it is better for me to die than to live.*

LXX: *O Lord, is this not what I said when I was still in my country? This is why I made haste to flee to Tarshish. For I know that you are rich in mercy and are kind, patient, and full of compassion, and ready to repent for the evils that you promised. But now all-powerful Lord, take my spirit, because it is better for me to die than to live.*

What I have interpreted as 'I pray you' and which the Septuagint has translated as 'O indeed'[1] is read as *anna* in Hebrew, which seems to me to express the prayer with a kind of coaxing. For when he had said quite justly that he wanted to flee his prayer accuses the Lord of injustice in a certain manner, and he tempers his complaints by a suppliant and rhetorical speech. Was this not what I said when I was in my country? I knew that you would do this. I am not unaware that you are merciful: this is why I refused to denounce you as harsh and cruel. Therefore I wanted to flee to Tarshish, to be free to think, and I preferred the quiet and rest on the sea of this age. I abandoned my home and left my inheritance, I left your lap and came here. If I had said that you are merciful, gentle, that you pardon wickedness, no one would have repented. If I had denounced you as a cruel God only fit to judge, I should have known that such is not your nature. In this dilemma I preferred to flee, rather than to deceive the repenters with mildness, or to preach things about you that you are not. "Therefore Lord take my spirit for death is better for me than life." (1 Kgs 19:4) "Take my spirit which has been sad even until death." (Mt. 26:38; Mk. 14:34) "Take my spirit. I place my spirit in your hands." (Ps. 30:6; Lk. 23:46) I was not able to save the whole nation of Israel by living, but I will die and the whole world will be saved. The story is clear and regarding the prophet's character, we can note as has often been said before that he is saddened and wants to die so that Israel should not be destroyed for ever after the conversion of such a multitude of Gentiles.

4:4 *Then said the LORD, Do you well to be angry?*

LXX: *The Lord replied to Jonah, are you so much afflicted?' The Hebrew word hara lach can be translated as 'are you annoyed?' and are you afflicted?*

And each one pertains to the prophet and to the Lord: either he is annoyed and fears appearing a liar to the inhabitants of Nineveh, or he is afflicted, knowing that Israel is going to be destroyed. And with reason God does not say to him: 'you are wrong to get angry' or 'to be afflicted', not wanting to reprehend one suffering, nor does he say, 'you have reason to be angry or afflicted', so as not to contradict his former sentence. But he asks him whether he is angry or afflicted so that he replies the causes of his anger or suffering, or even, if he remains quiet, so that God's truth can be proved by his silence.

4:5 *So Jonah went out of the city, and sat on the east side of the city, and there made him a booth, and sat under it in the shadow, till he might see what would become of the city.*

LXX: similar.

Cain who initiated civilization by fratricide and homicide in killing his brother was the first to build a city, and he gave it the name of his son Enoch. (Gen. 4:17) This is why the prophet Hosea declares, "I am God, and not a man, amongst you I am a saint, and I will not come into the city". (Hos. 11:9) For the Lord, says the psalmist, is the charge of "the transition of the dead" (Ps. 67:21). This is why one of this cities of refuge is called Ramoth (Deut. 4:43), which is translated as 'vision of death'. Therefore quite justly anyone who is a fugitive and on account of his sins does not merit living in Jerusalem lives in the city of death and is across the waves of the Jordan, which signifies 'descent'. The dove, or the suffering, comes out from such a town and lives in the east whence the sun rises. And it is there in his tent, where having contemplated every hour that passes, he hears what is going to happen to this city. Before Nineveh was saved and before the gourd dried up, before the Gospel of Christ becomes famous and the prophecy of Zechariah is realized: "here is a man whose name is East" (Zec. 6:12), Jonah was under his shelter. And nor had Truth come, about which the apostle of the Gospel says: "God is truth" (Jn. 3:33; 14:6; 1 Jn. 5:6), and he adds elegantly, "and he made there a shelter" near to Nineveh. He makes it himself, for no inhabitant of Nineveh of that age would have been able to live with the prophet, and he was seated under the

148

shade in the attitude of a judge or if you like, constrained by his majesty, "having pulled in vigorously his reins" (Prov. 31:17), so that his robe did not fall upon his feet and upon us who are low down, but was held together by a straighter belt. More precisely with regard to what he says, "to see what would happen to the city", this uses the accustomed usage of recourse to Scriptures to preach to God about human feelings.

4:6 *And the LORD God prepared a gourd, and made it to come up over Jonah, that it might be a shadow over his head, to deliver him from his grief. So Jonah was exceeding glad of the gourd.*

LXX: *and the Lord commanded a gourd to grow up over the head of Jonah to form a shade to protect him from his evils. And Jonah was very glad of the gourd indeed.*

In this place a certain Canterius from the ancient family of Cornelii, (or as he himself says from the lineage of Asinius Pollion), has accused me recently, it seems, of sacrilege for having translated 'ivy' instead of 'gourd'. Apparently he feared that if ivy were taken instead of gourds that there would not be anything to drink in his secret place and his shade. And justly on the veins of this gourd, which are called *saucomariae* in general, it is customary to paint the image of the Apostles from which this individual has borrowed his name, which is not his own. If it is this easy to change ones name, (after having been the Cornelii, seditious consuls, they renamed themselves Paul Emile consuls), I ask myself why in surprise I should not be allowed to translate ivy instead of gourd. But let us return to more serious matters. For gourd or ivy in Hebrew we read *qiqaion*, which is also written *qiqaia* in the Syriac and Punic languages. It is a type of shrub or sapling with wide leaves like a vine, and which casts a large shadow and is supported by a trunk and often is found growing in Palestine especially in sandy areas. It is interesting to note that if the seed is cast on the ground it germinates quickly and in a few days it can be seen to have grown from a seedling to a bush. For my part when I was translating the prophets I wanted to just transliterate the Hebrew word seeing that Latin has no word for this kind of tree. But I feared that the men of letters would find in this some argument, imagining those animals of India or the mountains of Boeotia or even other marvels of this type. I have also followed the example of the former translators who translated it as ivy, in Greek *chissos*, because they had no other word to use. let us now look carefully at the story, and having looked at the mythical meaning then go on to study each word individually. The gourd and the ivy creep along the ground by their nature, and if they have no restraints or ladders as support they do not try to climb. How is it possible then that a gourd could grow up without the prophet knowing in one night to provide shade, if its nature is not to climb unless it has some supports, reeds or pegs to hold on to? Although the gourd, offering a miracle in its sudden appearance, and showing the power of God in the protection of a leafy shade, was only following its own nature. Even this though can refer tothe person of the Lord Savior, let us not completely abandon our gourd on account of our *philocholochunthon*, so that we remember that passage of Isaiah, which says, "and the daughter of Zion is left as a cottage in a vineyard, or as a lodge in a garden of cucumbers, as a besieged city." (Is. 1:8) And because we do not find a gourd mentioned elsewhere in the Scriptures let us say then that where the cucumber grows gourds usually grow too. And Israel is compared to this kind of plant because, at a certain time, it protected Jonah with its shadow whilst he was waiting the conversion of the gentiles and made him feel greatly happy. It made more a shady shelter for him rather than a house, and that suggests a roof of some kind but not having the foundations of a house. Moreover the gourd, our little bush, which grows quickly and dries quickly, could be compared to Israel, pushing its little roots into the ground and trying to raise itself up, but is not able to equal the height of cedars (Ps. 79:11) and cypress trees (Is. 37:24; Zec. 11:2) of God. It seems to me that one could interpret the locusts that were food for John similarly, who said symbolizing Israel, "It must grow but I must die" (Jn. 3:30). The locust, a small animal with weak wings managing to rise up from the ground but not able to fly very high so that it is better called a reptile yet not similar either to birds.

4:7 *But God prepared a worm when the morning rose the next day, and it smote the gourd that it withered. And it came to pass, when the sun did arise, that God prepared a vehement east wind; and the sun beat upon the head of Jonah, that he fainted, and wished in himself to die, and said, it is better for me to die than to live.*

LXX: *and God commanded a worm early the next morning, which smote the gourd that it withered. When the sun had risen the Lord immediately commanded a hot and burning wind. The sun hit upon Jonah's head in his distress and suddenly became very exhausted and he said, it is better for me to die than to live.*

Before the sun of justice (Mal. 4:2) rose the shade was verdant and Israel was not dry. But after it rose, and when the darkness of Nineveh had been dispersed by its light, a worm obtained for the first light of the next day smote the gourd, (the worm, which is mentioned in the title to psalm twenty-one: "in honor of the morning incarnation", and which was born from the earth without any seed, can say, 'I am a worm and not a man' (Ps. 21:7). And Jonah, abandoned by God's aid, loses all his strength. The Lord ordered a hot and burning wind, which was prophesied by Hosea: "the Lord will bring a wind out of the desert, which will dry up the rivers and abandon his fountain" (Hos. 13:15). And Jonah began to get hot and once again he wants to die in the baptism of Israel to receive in this basin the moisture which he lost in his refusal to do God's word. This is why Peter speaks to the Jews who are parched, saying, "Repent, and let each of you be baptized in the name of Jesus Christ for payment for your sins, so that you might receive the gift of the Holy Spirit" (Act.). There are those for whom the worm and the burning wind represent the Roman generals who, after the resurrection of Christ, completely destroyed Israel.

4:9 *And God said to Jonah, Do you well to be angry for the gourd? And he said, I do well to be angry, even unto death.*

LXX: *and the Lord God said to Jonah, are you so afflicted for a gourd? He replied, 'I am very afflicted even to the point of death.*

151

When he was asked about the repentance of the inhabitants of Nineveh and the safety of the city of the Gentiles, 'do you well to be angry?', the prophet replied nothing, yet justified God's question by his silence. For he knew that God is kind, merciful, patient, and full of pity (Ex. 34:6; Ps. 102:8), pardoning wickedness and he did not feel sad for the safety of the gentiles; but once the gourd, (Israel) had dried up, when he is asked, 'do you well to be angry for the gourd?', he replies with assurance, 'I do well to be angry and to suffer even unto death. I did not want to save one only to see the others perish, to gain foreigners only to lose my own'. And in truth up until this day Christ weeps for Jerusalem and he weeps until death; not his own death, but that of the Jews, so that they die refusing and rise up again confessing the Son of God.

4:10-11 *Then said the LORD, You have had pity on the gourd, for the which you have not labored, neither made it grow; which came up in a night, and perished in a night: and should not I spare Nineveh, that great city, wherein are more than six score thousand persons that cannot discern between their right hand and their left hand; and also much cattle?*

LXX: *and the Lord said, 'you wanted to keep safe a gourd which has done you no wickedness, that you have not cared for, which was born in one night and died in one night. But should I not spare Nineveh the great city in which live over three thousand people who are unknowing of their right and their left, and an equal number of cattle?*

It is too difficult to explain how according to tropology this is said to the Son of man: 'you worry for a gourd that has done you no harm, that you did not plant' (Jn. 1:3), since all has been done by him and with him absent nothing has been done. This is why someone interpreting this passage and wanting to resolve the question which he asked himself, fell into blasphemy. For, if we look at the text of the Gospel, which says, "why do you call me good? Nothing is good except God himself." (Mk. 10:18) He interprets the Father as good and places the Son one place lower, in a comparison with one who is perfectly and completely good. And he has not seen that this opinion made him fall

152

into the heresy of Marcion, who proposes a God that is uniquely good, with another for judging and for creating, rather than the opinion of Arius who proposed a superior Father and an inferior Son yet admits the Son as creator. We must be indulgent therefore for that which we are about to say, and our attempts ought to be encouraged with good criticism and prayer, rather than declaimed by an argumentative audience. Criticism and declamation are easy for those who are most ignorant, but one must be learned and know the labors of workers to stretch out ones hand to those weaker or to show the way to those who are lost. Our Lord and Savior did not work for Israel as for the people of the gentiles. In this instance Israel declares in faith, "Look these many years do I serve you, neither transgressed I at any time thy commandment: and yet you never gave me a kid, that I might make merry with my friends: But as soon as this thy son was come, which hath devoured thy living with harlots, you have killed for him the fatted calf." (Lk. 15:29-32) And in spite of all he is not reprimanded by the Father, but he says to him kindly, "Son, you art ever with me, and all that I have is thine. It was meet that we should make merry, and be glad: for this thy brother was dead, and is alive again; and was lost, and is found." The fat calf has been slaughtered for the people of the gentiles, and its precious blood has been spread about, about which Paul to the Hebrews (9 and 10) explains in great detail. And David in the psalm says, "the brother does not redeem, man will redeem" (Ps. 48:8). Christ decided that this people would be great and he died so that they might live; he went down to the underworld so that this people might rise up to heaven. For Israel there is no

comparable toil. This is why he is jealous of his young brother, seeing that after having spent his fortune on his prostitutes and pimps, he receives the ring and the robe and recovers his former dignity. The phrase 'which was born in one night' can be applied to the time just before the arrival of Christ, who was the light of the world (Jn. 8:12; 9:5), about which is said, "the night has passed, and the day is near" (Rom. 13:12). And this people died in one night when the sun of righteousness (Mal. 4:2) set for them, and they lost the word of God. The city of Nineveh which is great and very beautiful, prefigures the Church in which there is a greater number of inhabitants than the ten tribes of Israel: this is what the rest of the twelve baskets in the desert represent (Mat. 14:20; Mk. 6:43; Lk. 9:17; Jn. 6:13). "they do not know the difference between their right and their left", either on account of their innocence and their simplicity (to show first childhood and let it be known what the number of those is who have reached an older age, when the very young are so numerous), or even, (because the city was great, and "in a great house there are not only golden and silver objects but also some made of wood and pottery" (2 Tim. 2:20) because there was a great crowd that needed to repent and was ignorant of the difference between good and bad, between their right and left. And there is a great number of animals and of men who do not possess the faculty of reason and who can be compared to mad animals to whom they are similar. (Ps. 48:21)

BIBLIOGRAPHY OF WORKS

· Antin, Dom Paul. Sur Jonah, Sources Chretiennes, Paris 1956

· Lewis, C.T. Elementary Latin Dictionary, OUP. 1997

· Kittel, R. Biblica Hebraica Stuttgartensia, Stuttgart, 1990

· Limburg, J Jonah, A commentary, John Knox, 1989

· Wollf. H.W. Obadiah and Jonah, A commentary, Augsburg, 1986

www.ingramcontent.com/pod-product-compliance
Lightning Source LLC
Chambersburg PA
CBHW081425090426

42740CB00017B/3189